# Global Security Paradoxes

## 2000-2020

*By the same Author*

1. **Restructuring Pakistan**
*(ISBN: 81-7049-134-7). Rs. 595/-*

2. **Restructuring South Asian Security**
*(ISBN: 81-7049-121-5). Rs. 495/-*

3. **Dealing with Global Terrorism**
The Way Forward
*(ISBN: 81-207-2534-4). Rs. 600/-*

4. **Third Millennium Equipoise**
*(ISBN: 1-897829-48-5). Rs. 395/-*

# Global Security Paradoxes

## 2000-2020

Major General Vinod Saighal

**Manas Publications**
**New Delhi - 110002**

**Manas Publications**
(Publishers, Distributors, Importers & Exporters)
4858, Prahlad Street
24, Ansari Road, Darya Ganj,
New Delhi - 110 002 (INDIA)
**Ph.: 23260783, 23265523 (O); 27131660 (R)**
**Fax: 011 - 23272766**
**E-mail: manaspublications@vsnl.com**
**www.manaspublications.com**



First Published 2004

**ISBN** 81-7049-194-0
Rs 595/-



Typeset at
Manas Publications

Printed in India at
Nice Printing Press
and Published by Mrs. Suman Lata for
**Manas Publications**, 4858, Prahlad Street
24, Ansari Road, Daryaganj
New Delhi 110002 (INDIA)

# Preface

As the book *Global Security Paradoxes (2000-2020)* goes into print, the world is already nearing the mid-point of the opening decade of the new century. In some respects the first few years have been as cataclysmic as the collapse of the Berlin Wall towards the close of the earlier century; the event that saw the dwindling of the superpower that had pinned its faith on communism as an opposing ideology to unbridled capitalism. Strangely enough, the remaining superpower, at its zenith, might be setting in motion a chain of events that could see it dwindle to the same extent as its erstwhile opponent in time frames that do not go beyond the ken of a generation or two.

The interplay of nations for domination or plain aggrandisement has been the norm throughout history. The present decade, however, is seeing tectonic shifts that could hardly have been thought possible just a few years ago. One of the profound changes could be the fading out of the most enduring relationships of the last century, the

Anglo-American entente, which seemed up to last year as solid as the proverbial Rock of Gibraltar. Although the residual momentum of the most stable relationship of the last century may keep it going a few more years due to the institutional urge of the support structures of the British establishment, public opinion in Britain has definitely turned against USA; possibly as solidly as in France, Germany, Russia, or even some of the Muslim countries. The import of this shift should not be lost upon the world. Hardly anyone in their wildest dreams could have imagined that an incumbent US President visiting Britain would face from Londoners implacable hostility of a type that the English have not shown in living memory to any visiting head of state. One writer likened George W. Bush's passage through London to a funeral cortège. What it means is that in a few years the British public will ally itself more solidly with continental Europe and shed its hangover of the special Anglo-American concord that endured for a century. In the process Europe will be immeasurably strengthened. And when the UK finally changes course, most nations that have sided with America, mainly on the coat tails of the British, will also go along with the new direction taken by the British people. America's ability to create a permanent divide in Europe and thereby prevent a European super state emerging as a counterweight rested squarely on British support. It will suffer diminishment. Europe's time is nigh. Incredibly, this second—and stronger—cohesion of Europe, anathema to US establishments, would have been brought about by the policies of a US President.

Britain is not the only case of a fundamental power shift that is taking place. Another paradox relates to Turkey.

Turkey was one of the strongest pillars of NATO till the collapse of the Soviet Empire. Inspite of that break up Turkey remained steadfast in its commitment to the West. Having contributed so handsomely to the strength of the Western alliance for over 50 years it took for granted that sooner or later it would find its place in the European Union. In the last few years, when it started becoming apparent to the Turks that they were being put on the backburner for EU membership, while the former communist countries of East Europe were being moved fast forward, they never really abandoned hope of ultimately joining the EU. Turkey's strongest proponents in this endeavour were the USA and UK, who kept pushing for early Turkish membership of the EU. Ironicallly, after the US intervention in Iraq - and irrespective of the policies adopted by the Turkish government and the generals - the fact remains that anti-Americanism is fast becoming as strong in Turkey as anywhere else in the Muslim world. If anything, the hostile sentiment could grow stronger in the coming years. In the face of this paradox, it remains a moot point whether the USA would still remain a strong backer of Turkish membership of EU. Going a step further, when the US realizes that hatred for USA is deeply embedded in Turkey, would it be comfortable with the thought of 70 million Turks, the vast majority hostile to the US, being full citizens of the EU? The significance of the shift could hardly be lost upon the EU or the USA.

There are other paradoxes that have been reflected in the book, most importantly the change that is taking place in Russia. The Russia of 2004 is a far cry from the wilting Russia of the Yeltsin years, when the Western nations led by USA moved in for the proverbial kill. In a short span of time under the firm hand of Vladimir N. Putin, Russia is again rising phoenix-like from the ashes to stand up and be counted as a world power, if not yet again a matching superpower. What the future unfolds for Russia and the world is difficult to tell. The chapter 'Resurgence of Russia in the 21st Century' is indicative of the changes that might come about.

**Vinod Saighal**

# List of Acronyms

| | |
|---|---|
| ABM | Anti Ballistic Missile (Treaty entered into between USSR and USA in 1972) |
| ABC | Asian Brown Cloud |
| AIDS | Acquired Immune Deficiency Syndrome |
| BMD | Ballistic Missile Defence |
| BIMARU | Bihar, Madhya Pradesh, Rajasthan, Uttar Pradesh (States in India). |
| CAR | Central Asian Republics |
| CBW | Chemical or Biological Weapons |
| CIS | Commonwealth of Independent States |
| CTBT | Comprehensive Test Ban Treaty |
| ECM | Electronic Counter Measures |
| ECCM | Electronic Counter Counter Measures |
| EKV | Exo-atmospheric Kill Vehicle |
| GDP | Gross Domestic Product |

| | |
|---|---|
| GPC | Global Population Commission |
| IAEA | International Atomic Energy Agency |
| ICBM | Intercontinental Ballistic Missile |
| IR | Infra-red |
| ISI | Inter-Services Intelligence (Directorate of Pakistan) |
| LTTE | Liberation Tigers of Tamil Eelam |
| MALD | Miniature Air-launched Decoys |
| MDA | Missile Defence Agency |
| Milsat | Military Satellite |
| MQM | Muhajir Qaumi Muteheda (commonly referred to as Mohajir Qaumi Movement) |
| NATO | North Atlantic Treaty Organisation |
| NFU | No-First-Use |
| NMD | National Missile Defence |
| NPP | National Population Policy |
| NTW | Navy Theatre Wide |
| PNE | Peaceful Nuclear Explosion |
| R&D | Research & Development |
| RAID | Rapid Assessment and Initial Detection |
| RMA | Revolution in Military Affairs |
| SCO | Shanghai Cooperation Organization |
| SDI | Strategic Defence Initiative |
| TAR | Tibet Autonomous Region |
| THAAD | Theater High-Altitude Area Defence |

| | |
|---|---|
| TMD | Theatre Missile Defence |
| UCAV | Uninhabited Combat Air Vehicle |
| UNEP | United Nations Environment Programme |
| UNESCO | United Nations Educational, Scientific and Cultural Organisation |
| UNSC | United Nations Security Council |
| USAF | United States Air Force |
| WHO | World Health Organisation |
| WMD | Weapons of Mass Destruction |

# Contents

# Introduction

Many of the issues dealt with in this book have sufficient global import to last beyond the first two decades of the new century. The manner in which they are addressed could propel the world into a *cul-de-sac* where the way is permanently barred at one end and retracing steps at the other becomes improbable. The abrogation of the 1972 ABM Treaty with Russia by the Bush administration is a case in point. The treaty had been pivotal to the post-Cold War stability and the non-militarisation of space. The actions of George W. Bush should have convinced the world that not only was the USA not going to abide by several painstakingly negotiated protocols, it could through its policies accelerate the forces of terror and disruption throughout the world. Exorbitant outlays that would be required to underpin the National Missile Defence Programme over several decades could end up by siphoning off tens of billions of dollars from productive purposes – both within USA and globally—towards potentially destabilizing ends. While the full maturation of the NMD programme with sufficiently high probability of interception to warrant the fantastic outlays could end up costing anything up to half a trillion dollars over the useful life of the programme, the results would hardly be commensurate with the effort or expense. Forces inimical to USA around the world after having been 'zapped' by US high-tech warfare on several occasions since the First Gulf War have become conscious of the power asymmetries in play. They are well on the way to finding alternatives to defeat these technologies. Similarly, the NMD umbrella simply beckons those forces to take its toll of US interests by remaining *under* the umbrella. The ICBM route to destruction and counter destruction was a relic of the Cold War. America's opponents have grasped this fact. US lobbies sucking out US capital will not allow the American people to face up to the new reality.

At the other end of the very high-tech spectrum, Russia is planning to build a more powerful nuclear-tipped missile, which it is claimed will ensure strategic parity with the United States. The new long-range missile being designed will be armed with ten nuclear warheads, powered by a liquid fuel engine that will enable it to carry up to four tonnes of payload. Earlier, Russia had inducted six new Topol-M nuclear missiles. At an induction ceremony broadcast by Russian television stations on 21 December 2003, the Defence Minister, Sergei Ivanov called it the most advanced state-of-the-art missile in the world. He went on to add 'only such weapons can guarantee our sovereignty and security and make any attempts to put military pressure on Russia absolutely senseless'. The 47-ton 18-metre Topol-M missile, capable of hitting targets more than 10,800 km away, is said to be a full generation ahead of US missiles and *cannot* be shot down either by existing or future anti-missile systems. It is also immune to electronic jamming. To date, Russia had been deploying the silo-based single-warhead Topol-M missiles. Its mobile version armed with four to six warheads and mounted on a heavy off-road vehicle, is set to become operational in the near future according to the spokesman of the Russian General Staff. By 2012, Russia will have somewhere between 1700 to 2200 nuclear warheads on its long-range missiles, the maximum arsenal allowed under the Russian-American Strategic Weapons Treaty signed in May 2002.[1]

Creeping loss of sovereignty is taking place in many parts of the world, mostly due to market capitalism in full cry, linked to the US expansionist urge. Latin America had always known that the Monroe Doctrine of the USA was not merely designed to keep the rest of the world out, it *ipso facto* implied abridgement of the national sovereignty of these countries. After the end of the Cold War, the USA is assiduously extending a variation of the doctrine to the Middle East and a few other countries in Central and South Asia, ostensibly as part of its drive to counter global terrorism. Iraq, Afghanistan and Pakistan fall in this category. In the case of Pakistan, its military dictators – the present incumbent or successors—may continue to rail against India in whatever form; their freedom of manoeuvre, however, would remain limited to mischief in Jammu & Kashmir. With the spread of the weapons of mass destruction to a number of states that have been classified as 'rogue states', the USA could hardly be unmindful of the fact that the capacities of almost all these states have been built up through clandestine transfers from Pakistan. Therefore, while steps are being taken to roll back the WMD capabilities of Iran, Libya and North Korea, the USA would certainly be taking steps to ensure that it gets a grip on Pakistan's nuclear capabilities, more so if there is a chance of their falling into the hands of non-state actors. As matters stand, the most likely source for acquisition of WMD capability by non-state actors remains Pakistan and North Korea, solidly allied in the enhancement of each other's nuclear and missile capabilities.

Potentially the most promising development on the global horizon, besides the ongoing movement towards a more *independent* and *integrated* European Union, is the promise of the emergence of China as a responsible member of the global community in the 21st century. Today the growing Chinese economy confers upon Chinese leaders a self-assurance that was lacking in the second half of the preceding century. Its phenomenal economic growth automatically pushes China to the front rank of countries shaping the world in the ensuing decades. China's pragmatism in foreign affairs, which could be inferred by some as yielding ground to USA, might not only be due to the perceived gap in military strength between the two countries. It is more likely to be the case that China sees itself becoming the dominant player on the global economic template well before the middle of the new century, overtaking in the process the economic giants of the earlier decades, USA, Japan and Europe. For achieving these ends, peace in Asia, especially east of the 76º meridian becomes an essential prerequisite. Hence, accommodation with India on the boundary question as well as on the question of support to Pakistan is likely to become one of the important foreign policy goals for China. A historic *rapprochement* along these lines would benefit both countries enormously. Tentative steps towards this end have already been taken.

Many people may still feel that Pakistan, whom the Chinese leaders have often termed as the 'all weather friend of China', might be able to act as a spoiler in the improvement of relations between China and India. In all likelihood, China has already moved beyond that stage without Pakistan realizing it. It is unlikely that the deep-seated mutual respect that marked relations between the two ancient civilizations for centuries on end could have been marred by the relatively recent geopolitical alignments that can be seen to have been a hangover of the Cold War years. Regardless of what might have happened in the past, hereafter, China is not likely to part with nuclear technologies to Pakistan. Just as the Americans and many other countries have realized that Pakistan's internal cohesion has been hopelessly impaired by the military regime and the rise of Islamic fundamentalism, China too has become apprehensive about the fallout of a failed Pakistan state should it come about; or for that matter the gradual takeover of some, if not all, of the levers of Pakistan's governance mechanisms by the theology-centered polity, which has been brought to the fore by the compulsions of Pakistan's military dictators for holding on to power. In the process it has buried the democratic urges of the Pakistani civil society.

A large number of articles have been written by US commentators on European Union integration and the attempts by France and Germany for the setting up of an independent defence capability. It would not be an exaggeration to state that almost every single article on the subject by an American goes against the spirit of European unity as perceived by the prime movers of European unification in continental Europe, i.e. Germany, France and the BENELUX countries. Right from the time that communism took root in the Soviet Union since the end of World War I the Western nations have been solidly allied to USA. The relationship was further cemented with the setting up of NATO after World War II. Only a few years ago it would have been inconceivable to think that USA and Europe, at least Western Europe, could drift apart. That is precisely what is happening, possibly irreversibly so.

The sooner the Americans realize it, the better for them. Regardless of the impediments created in its path and the delays caused by US policies to divide Europe, the movement, however slow, can only be in the direction indicated from Paris, Berlin, Belgium and Luxembourg. At heart, irrespective of the contrary policies of some of their leaders, notably in UK, Spain, Italy, Poland and some of the other East European countries, the people of Europe across the board would like to see the emergence of a strong independent Europe. A Europe that values its ties to the USA, yet remains sufficiently free from blind adherence to US policies that are clearly not in Europe's interest.

US indebtedness remains a cause for worry—for the remainder of the world as well as for the Americans. If the policies pursued by the US administration are not radically reformed – economic as well as geopolitical policies – the USA could sink deeper into indebtedness. Presently, few expect a reprieve for the dollar, with some economic experts maintaining that a combination of very low US interest rates and a strong global recovery will make it even harder for the US to attract enough capital to offset its current account deficit. Apparently, the current account deficit becomes a long-term factor, while the fundamental driver of the weakness of the dollar remains strong.

Like in the case of adverse situations that get worse with the passage of time unless drastic remedial measures are put into effect, the prospects for US recovery from indebtedness do not look bright. When irremediable financial crisis finally overtakes it, the USA, in the fashion of imperial powers throughout history would be tempted to come out of its financial predicament by conquests. Whenever Rome's financial condition became precarious, ancient Rome sent its legions into Asia to plunder the wealth of the lands across the seas. This happened not once, but many times. Other empires that followed did the same. What needs to be remembered is that after Iraq the world may no longer acquiesce in the manner that it did on the earlier occasion. It would be in everybody's interest if realization were to dawn on the US public that the sooner the Americans trim their sails, the better it would be for America - and the world.

Before the year 2003 ended, Iran signed a protocol giving the UN nuclear watchdog, the International Atomic Energy Agency (IAEA) the right to conduct snap inspections of its atomic facilities. Unlike the previous IAEA, UN Security Council mandate to conduct weapons inspections in pre-war Iraq, the protocol does not give the IAEA the right to carry out unannounced 'anywhere and anytime' inspections in Iran. It did, however, give the agency the right to demand much more information about sensitive nuclear activities and to inspect all declared and undeclared nuclear sites with as little as two hours notice.[2]

Any discussion on the global security paradoxes in the opening decade of the century would be incomplete without a reference to the US intervention in Iraq. As volumes have already been written about it since the intervention took place and several tomes are bound to follow in the coming years, a passing reference to highlight aspects relevant to the present discourse will suffice for the purpose of this book. The first relates to the Blue Ribbon Panel set up by the UN Secretary General in November 2003 to go into aspects that could propel the world towards collective security as distinct from US unilateralism that has shaken the world order. While not going deeply into the terms of reference, it can be mentioned in passing that they may not serve the desired ends as they do not go far enough in *confronting* the challenge to the world order posed by resurgent US imperialism. The second and more immediate aspect concerns US attempts to remould Iraq after the fashion legislated in Washington. It does not come as a surprise to onlookers that the US might not find it easy to usher in the type of democracy that suits US interests while ignoring those of the Iraqi people or Iraq's neighbours in the region.

In this regard it would be interesting to go back to an interview given in March 2003 by Vice President Dick Cheney.[3] In the course of the interview the Vice President accused the Iraqi strongman of actively pursuing the acquisition of nuclear weapons and with having long-standing ties to Al-Qaeda and so on. An impression also emerged that the military conquest of Iraq would not be difficult and that when the Americans went in the Iraqi people would greet them as liberators. The interviewer challenging Cheney's rosy forecast put the question: "If your analysis is not correct, and we're not treated as liberators, but conquerors, and the Iraqis begin to resist, particularly in Baghdad, do you think the American people are prepared for a long, costly, and bloody battle with significant American casualties?"

This episode clearly shows that not only was disinformation fed to the world by the US and British establishments, as is now abundantly clear, it is also becoming apparent that in the process these very establishments managed to delude themselves to a similar degree. So hell-bent were they upon the conquest of Iraq that they did not take the elementary steps necessary for preventing Iraq from descending into administrative collapse after victory had been achieved.

Flowing from this, details have appeared in a US magazine[4] of Donald Rumsfeld, the US Defence Secretary on a visit to Iraq toward the end of 2003 grilling the 4th Infantry Division Commander in his command post near Kirkuk. "What's happened since I was here (in September)?" Rumsfeld demands to know. Odierno (the divisional commander) rattles off an answer, but the flak intensifies. "How many people are you capturing or killing a week?" Rumsfeld asks. "Two hundred captured, up to 100 killed", Odierno responds. "Of those captured, how many do you throw back?" Rumsfeld asks. "Ten percent" Odierno replies. Rumsfeld: "And the rest we're locking up?" "We've locked up probably over 4,000, sir".

Just *one* divisional commander admits that his troops are killing nearly 100 Iraqis a week. By straightforward extrapolation it can be worked out that at a minimum between 500 to 1000 Iraqis are being killed every week all over Iraq and possibly twice that number being detained – often for indeterminate periods. On a monthly basis, it could work out to approximately 2000 to 3000 Iraqis being killed. The annual figure would reach nearly 40,000 killed and anything up to 100,000 incarcerated. Whichever way one looks at it, it adds up to phenomenal bloodletting by the occupation forces of a captive people *after* the war was officially declared over. The extrapolation is based on figures given out. Clandestinely, the number of Iraqis being killed through indirect US action is anybody's guess. The deaths occurring through the action of fellow Iraqis against coalition forces or those backing coalition forces would again be large. The figures do not include deaths taking place for various reasons directly attributable to the destruction caused by the Anglo-US intervention i.e. non-availability of health care, medicines, infrastructure breakdown and the like. Saddam Hussein, the tyrant has been accused of genocide. The category in which the post-Saddam deaths in Iraq should be classified becomes a fit case for consideration by the UN General Assembly or the Blue Ribbon Panel appointed by the UN Secretary General.

Possibly the most significant paradox of the age relates to global terrorism versus faith in non-violent struggles. The world has been so inured to the China, Tibet, India equation of the previous century that it failed to take into account the importance of perhaps one of the most important developments of recent years as it moved into the new century. The epochal event that needs to be highlighted is that in spite of the repression visited upon the hapless Tibetan nation since the Chinese invaded Tibet, the Dalai Lama has remained steadfast in his belief in non-violence. Any other leader, recoiling in horror at the magnitude of the devastation wrought on his people, would long ago have changed course; in the manner of so many insurgent and terrorist organizations that have sprung up all over the world to cause a veritable nightmare for the well-being of so many nations.

## End Notes

1. *The Hindu,* 23 December 2003.
2. *Reuters.* Reproduced in *The Statesman,* 19 December 2003.
3. *NBC News,* "Meet the Press" show, 16 March 2003, interview with Tim Russert. <www.larouchein2004.com>
4. *TIME,* 29 December 2003 / 5 January 2004.

# 1

# *A Critique of the Military Dimension of South Asian Security

The prevailing situation has forced many nations, treaty organisations and regional groupings around the world to reevaluate and possibly restructure their security perspectives. There is general acceptance all around that the security dimension has to be seen in its totality to embrace, *inter alia*, the socio-economic domain. Further, regardless of where a nation happens to be situated geographically it cannot really plan for its security without taking into account the altered global reality that intruded rudely on the global consciousness on September 11, 2001.

Inevitably, while in the changed world order oil-related geo-economics has assumed as great an importance as was the case with geopolitics of yesteryear there is no gainsaying that in the present context the military dimension might continue to preponderate for the foreseeable future over the socio-economic, environmental and allied dimensions in the national and regional security perspectives of South

---

* Based on talks delivered at: North Eastern Hill University (NEHU), Shillong in August 2003; Institute for International and Security Affairs, Berlin in September 2003; Lal Bahadur Shastri National Academy of Administration, Mussoorie in December 2003.

Asia. Since the epicenter of global terrorism that manifested itself on September 11, and December 13, 2001 in continental USA and in New Delhi respectively, happened to be the Pakistan-Afghanistan region it becomes almost *de rigeur* for any critique of the military dimension of South Asian security to lay emphasis on those aspects of global terrorism that have led to the injection of outside military forces into the South Asian region and its neighbourhood; for a stay that may not be vacated any time in the near future.

As a corollary thereto, it becomes essential to try and look into those areas of regional security which, should they become stabilizing factors contributing tc regional and global security, could lead to a diminishment of the extra-territorial military presence in Afghanistan, Pakistan and Central Asia. A thought has also to be given to the potential for regional stability (long-term) and regional instability (short-term) that may incidentally ensue from the US intervention in Afghanistan, Iraq and the US-led build up in the region. Much, of course, will depend upon the outcome of the intervention in Iraq and increasingly in Afghanistan as well.

The point to be noted is that the factors relating to national security become variables: in relation to space (geographical location); time (whether there is stability in the region during that period); the attitude of the superpower (USA) towards the countries concerned; the hostility of the neighbours (or otherwise); the internal security situation; economic vulnerability; social equilibrium and a host of other factors.

## EXTERNALITIES THAT IMPINGE ON THE SOUTH ASIAN SECURITY ENVIRONMENT

Currently, if looked at purely from the point of regional stability in and around Afghanistan, the US military presence is crucial to peace in the region till at least the time that an effective and stable government in control of the situation is in place in Afghanistan and an enduring democratic transition is effected in Pakistan. Should the USA limit its aims in the post-intervention phase to eliminating all vestiges of the ISI-Taliban–Al-Qaeda network and refrain from actions that could be viewed with concern by the other major regional powers like Russia and China, peace will return to the region. Any advancement of US geo-strategic aims through its present military deployment could lead to tensions in the years ahead. The bigger powers in the region would be wondering about the duration of the post-Afghanistan (and lately post-Iraq) intervention phase of the US presence in the region? Will the presence remain at the same level? Or will it be reduced? Or will it be augmented? In case of extended stay what would be the readjustments that the regional powers will have to carry out in the near future, as well as in the medium and long-terms – in their individual capacity, bilaterally, multilaterally and as a collectivity.

Since it was the events of the September 11, that changed the global order, one of the first questions that surfaces from the rubble of the WTC collapse concerns the intelligence failures that led to the attacks on the symbols of US might – both military and economic. Not only Americans, but also people around the world would be wondering as to how intelligence failures of such magnitude occurred. Could they occur again?

Had the ISI-Al-Qaeda network not targeted USA and had decided instead to restrict their activities to Europe, Russia, the subcontinent and elsewhere it is well on the cards that they would have done considerable damage worldwide while the USA simply looked on. It is also possible that such shifting of focus might not have yielded similar results due to the nature of the indoctrination carried out in the *madrasas* of Pakistan and Afghanistan. The hatred imbued into the young minds through slogans like 'death to America' and 'death to India' provided a well-defined focus for the people motivated to carry out the suicide attacks.

Since the Western alliance into which Japan has been co-opted is likely to remain in place in the ensuing decades the only potential challenge to a super dominant role of the US in every region of the world, notably Asia and Asia-Pacific, remains China. Regardless of the attempts at forming a more integrated China-Russia-India triangle none of these countries is seriously interested in setting up even a remotely confrontationist structure against the USA. Should the triangular relationship be formed, it would limit itself to providing some sort of counterbalance in the form of an identity of views against a US unilateralist approach; more specifically, those elements of unilateralism that are generally opposed by the world at large, including the European nations. Examples of such flying-in-the-face-of-the-world opinion relate to the 1972 ABM Treaty.

## THREATS TO SUBCONTINENTAL STABILITY

It is not the intention here to analyze each and every threat, military or otherwise, to India and the other nations of South Asia. Nor is it intended to go into the details of the violent movements that have taken a heavy toll of small-sized countries like Sri Lanka and Nepal. In the overall context, the major factor affecting South Asian harmonization has been the conflicts between India and Pakistan resulting from the partition of India in 1947. These conflicts resulted in major arms flows into both countries. It also led to an increase in military spending, especially in the case of Pakistan where the army usurped power for long periods of time. In the process, after meeting the defence expenditure and debt servicing, not much was left over for education, health or infrastructure development in Pakistan. This lack of availability of funds for improving the human condition has been a major factor contributing to the rise of fundamentalism in Pakistan and the region. In the case of Pakistan, it also led to the increase of Chinese and the other outside influences, including the flow of nuclear materials and missile technologies.

Hence, giving a more generalized treatment to the aspect of threat perceptions, these can be listed as: military threats; societal unrest attributable to an extent to lack of effective and impartial governance; rising levels of corruption; fiscal profligacy; population proliferation; large segments of the population remaining illiterate and below the poverty line; other socio-economic factors. As if these were not daunting enough prospects militating against socio-economic betterment and stability, there is now the added threat of a nuclear standoff.

While many of the threats listed above have across-the-board applicability at the present time – and the foreseeable future—there is a major environmental threat looming on the horizon that could prove catastrophic for the entire subcontinent and many of the countries of Southeast Asia. It concerns the massive deforestation, the frenetic pace of exploitation of natural resources and heavy militarisation of the Tibetan Plateau. These could result in climatic modifications threatening the very existence of South Asian and Southeast Asian societies. The inexorable consequences of the ecological ravaging of Tibet and the Himalayas could condemn the coming generations on the subcontinent, China and Southeast Asia to an existence far worse than is possible to imagine at this juncture, although the alarm signals are all there. The tragedy is that the civilization that prides itself as being the repository of the wisdom of the ages is ignoring it in a manner whose blindness is difficult to comprehend. It is worth dwelling on this aspect for a while and to examine the evidence:

- Many great river systems trace their source from the Tibetan Plateau, flowing into India, Pakistan, Bangladesh, Nepal, Bhutan, Myanmar, Thailand,

Vietnam, Cambodia, Laos and China. They water some of the most productive croplands in the world.

- The population of the area between the Yellow River in the east to the Indus in the west comprises nearly 47 per cent of the world's population.
- Over-exploitation of the fragile environment of Tibet and the Himalayas is leading to grave ecological devastation. Pollution at the headwaters of rivers in Tibet, including from nuclear wastes, is leading to serious ecological and biogenetic consequences.
- Massive deforestation, resulting from equally massive military deployments, has contributed significantly to siltation and destructive flooding in the Brahmaputra, Yangtse, Mekong, Indus, Sutlej, Salween and the Yellow Rivers. These rivers flow into the South China Sea, Bay of Bengal and the Arabian Sea. The global scale of these ecological disasters has yet to be fully assimilated.
- The Tibetan Plateau plays a critical role in the stability of the global climate and the monsoons.
- Himalayan glaciers are receding at a worrisome rate.

There has been talk that Chinese experts are considering the prospect of diversion of some of the waterways that flow into South and Southeast Asia through the use of peaceful nuclear explosions or atomic demolitions. Should they actually proceed in that direction due to the impending water scarcities it could spell doom for large sections of the populations of Pakistan, India, Bangladesh, and Southeast Asian countries. In the opinion of this writer the greatest threats to the stability and survivability of the subcontinent are: the long-term effects of Chinese activities in Tibet, the failure to check population growth, growing fundamentalism and possibility of economic decline of some of the states.

## THE USA FACTOR

Marching alone against a global consensus the US abrogated the 1972 ABM Treaty. The US already has the strongest military presence in the world. By deciding now to go in for a yet stronger shield, a unique one at that, it is forcing countries to redouble research into patterns of asymmetric warfare. It leaves countries like China—especially China—with little choice in the matter. The US should know that asymmetric warfare is what terrorists will thrive on in the future.

The essential strategic purpose of the American-led response to Islamic jehad could turn out to be both destruction and conquest. The response would be sufficiently long-term to make the undertaking successful. At the start of the global coalition against terror, put together by the US, the platform of common interests was more compelling than the differences that could, at a later stage, plague them bilaterally.

It has to be noted that in its initial response to global terrorism, after it was shaken to the core, the USA was willing, or at least appeared to be willing, to come close to the global fraternity to find common cause against what it considered to be a faceless enemy. At that point in time, not knowing what the faceless enemy would do next, the US manifested the symptoms of a responsible member of the global community. No sooner had it become clear that the Taliban and Al-Qaeda would be decisively defeated, it began to again display the arrogance of a superpower and global bully. A few days after the fall of Kandahar, President Bush announced his intention to walk out of the ABM Treaty with Russia.

After the first round victory in Afghanistan, the US did not dispel fears that its choice of terrorists elsewhere was determined by political convenience. It created the unmistakable impression that it could use the charge of terrorism to target all its adversaries. The world may be witnessing a permanent change in the character of US society. It has implications for Europe and the world.

Today, foreign policy in the US and geopolitics around the globe are no longer being conducted by people concerned about the welfare of nations or the stability of the new world order. In the region of turmoil i.e., Afghanistan and the countries around it, it is the US oil lobbies that have taken over the conduct of both foreign policy and military affairs. Their policies are a continuation of the accommodations arrived at with the Taliban and the US oil interests between the years 1996 and 1998. These interests, which have representation at the highest levels of the US establishment, appear to be convinced that they can exploit the oil and gas reserves in the Caspian basin, that are possibly the greatest source of untapped fossil fuels on earth, only if the pipeline runs through Afghanistan. Other configurations would dilute American control. The same logic extends to the Middle East and the intervention in Iraq.

## THE RUSSIA FACTOR

Russia gave its endorsement to President George W. Bush's strategy for fighting global terrorism without delay. Once US intervention commenced in Afghanistan and the outlines of the post-intervention strategies of the US and its allies started taking shape, President Putin might have had reasons for anxiety. Whatever the standpoint, a long-term convergence of interests in the region – as opposed to fighting global terrorism per se—between USA and Russia would seem unlikely. No doubt Russia had to pull back considerably from Central Asia after the collapse of the Soviet Union. In the Yeltsin years its economy had gone into a tailspin and the unrest in Russia itself hardly allowed any room for manoeuvre beyond Russia's borders. However, after a measure of stability had been attained under President Putin, Russia could not have for long ignored its interests in its immediate neighbourhood in Central Asia.

Being mindful of its reduced influence in world affairs and the precarious state of its economy Russia felt obliged to arrive at strategic accommodation with China. Therefore, while both these countries are quite alive to the problems posed by Islamic terrorism in their own countries they would not welcome a permanent US military presence in Central Asia or even Pakistan, for that matter.

Russia agreed to intelligence sharing and co-ordination of military strategies. Looking into the future Russia's plans for the Northern Alliance may not remain for long in total conformity with those of the USA. Certain commonalities would, nonetheless, remain. For both countries the Northern Alliance represents more than a trip-wire against resurgent Islamic fundamentalism spilling over into Central Asia, in the case of a revitalized post-Taliban force emerging again from the seminaries in Pakistan. Hence, both countries would realize that for the long-term the threat of Islamic fundamentalism emerges more from Pakistan than Afghanistan. The cohesion of the Northern Alliance is superficial. Its fissures could be deepened by an American backed Uzbekistan playing a lone hand through their protégé. The seeds of future discord have already been sown. Russia would be more inclined to co-ordinate its strategies with Iran. It becomes vital for both these countries to keep a firm grip on the situation in northern Afghanistan. As the Americans consolidate in Uzbekistan and the other Central Asian countries Moscow's wariness will increase. Uzbekistan, in return for support would expect financial help from USA as also help to fight the Islamic militants who have posed a big threat to the present regime.

Recent reports coming out from Russia reflect a desire for greater closeness with Western Europe. Taken to its logical conclusion these developments have the potential for becoming an important determinant of global stability in the coming decades.

## THE CHINA FACTOR

The growing desertification in China that threatens the livelihood of 35 million people across the north of the country could lead China to adopt policies in the coming decades that could lead to heightened tensions with its southern neighbours. Decades of rapid industrialization have resulted in environmental degradation. Nearly 20 percent of China's land territory has turned to desert because of natural and human factors. Overall desertification keeps on worsening. The nearest sand dune is less than 100 miles from Beijing. It is getting closer every year. Northern China has suffered increasingly frequent sandstorms turning day into night for a few hours as far away as South Korea. Soil erosion has led to huge farmland losses and the drying out of once mighty waterways such as the Yellow River. Desert land increases by 1,350 square miles every year, according to Zhou Shengxian, the Director of the State Forestry Administration. He said: "The reasons for the seemingly unstoppable process mostly relate to excessive human exploitation".[1]

Scientists are largely in agreement that China's dash for growth during the past two decades of economic reforms is to blame. There is a link between industrialization and desertification. It is poisoning the air and water. Many businesses dump toxic waste near their factories. As a result, trees and other vegetation die and soil erosion takes place. The rise of small private enterprise, embraced by millions, has led to further deforestation. Unless China radically reforms its economic and rapid, almost uninhibited industrialization policies, future generations in China might have to bear extraordinarily heavy existential costs. A lingering worry for South Asia would be the possibility of China transferring some of these costs to other nations through its activities in Tibet, which would adversely impact India and South Asia in a major way, should these projects fructify.

For example, waters of some of the world's greatest rivers are being diverted through very large-sized engineering projects. In what China claims to be the biggest engineering project of all time, it will divert part of the flow of the world's fourth-biggest river, the Yangtze in southern China, to replenish the Yellow River in the north, which is being drained dry. The first water from the $60 billion scheme could start flowing by the time Beijing hosts the Olympic games in 2008. Twenty years hence, when the project is completed it will siphon north around fifty cubic kilometres of water a year. It has far-reaching ramifications. China's "south-to-north" project follows hot on the heels of the Three Gorges dam on the Yangtze, the world's largest hydroelectric dam. The south-to-north project has three stages, each likely to match the Three Gorges for size and cost. The eastern arm of the new project will extract water from Jiangdu, near the mouth of the Yangtze. From there it will be carried along the 1500-year-old Grand Canal and under the Yellow River, to the water-starved city of Tianjin. The middle arm will begin at Danjiangkou, which will be enlarged—displacing 250,000 people—and flow down a new canal to Beijing. The third, western, arm is the biggest and most complex. It will capture the headwaters of the Yangtze in a 300-metre-high dam downstream from the melting glaciers of Tibet. Every year, it will lift a volume of water equivalent to a quarter of the annual flow of the river Nile through a 100-kilometre tunnel into the upper reaches of the Yellow River. Construction could start around 2010.

According to Wang Hao of the China Institute of Water Resources, China is suffering a hydrological crisis that leaves it no choice but to embark on such gigantic projects. Five times in the past decade, the 4800-kilometre-long Yellow River has failed to reach the sea for part of the year because every last drop has been diverted to irrigation channels and city taps. Parts of the river's parched upper basin are turning to desert, unleashing dust storms that occasionally reach all the way to Canada. In April 2003, as the growing season began, the river had its lowest spring flow for 50 years and irrigation channels dried up across 16 million hectares of fields. The aquifers of northern China are being depleted at a staggering rate of 30 cubic kilometres a year. In several places, 90 percent of the reserve is gone. The water table beneath Beijing has fallen 59 metres in the past 40 years. The north of China, which has two-thirds of the crop land but only one-fifth of the nation's water, needs 28 cubic kilometres more water each year. That figure will rise to 66 cubic kilometres by 2030, according to Wang. Even after completion of the south-to-north scheme, the region will still be short of 16 cubic kilometres a year.[2]

Against the background of the reports coming in of China planning to conduct feasibility study on power projects in Tibet, alarm bells automatically start ringing in India and other countries of South and Southeast Asia. With China mulling over the construction of a huge hydropower dam to tame river Brahmaputra that originates in Tibet, the water flow to India and Bangladesh could be affected. The Chinese section of the river, 2,057 kilometres long, boasts a water energy reserve of about 100 million kilowatts, or one-sixth of the country's total, ranking second behind the Yangtze. The location for the possible hydropower plant is the u-shaped turn of the river in the southeastern part of Tibet. The river drops 2,755 metres in the 500 kilometre-long "u" section, leading to a water energy reserve of about 68 million kilowatts, or one-tenth of the national total. "Yarlung Zangbo" is the Tibetan name for the Chinese section of the river Brahmaputra, which runs through India, and flows into the Indian Ocean in Bangladesh, where it is called Jamuna.[3]

The proposed power station is forecast to produce more than twice the electricity of the controversial Three Gorges

Dam being built on the Yangtze. The project, which also involves diverting Tibetan water to arid regions, is due to begin as soon as construction of the Three Gorges Dam is completed in 2009. China will have to overcome fierce opposition from neighbouring countries who fear that the scheme could endanger the lives and livelihoods of millions of their people. Critics say that those living downstream would be at the mercy of Chinese dam officials who would be able to flood them or withhold their water supply. International opposition may bar Beijing from World Bank loans for the project and prevent it from listing bonds and shares on world markets to fund the scheme. If, as its experts believe, China has to use nuclear materials in order to blast the proposed 10-mile tunnel, the country will attract international opprobrium for breaching the Comprehensive Test Ban Treaty.

Nuclear devices have been used in the past by Russia for engineering schemes, but the United States has rejected their use for civil projects on safety grounds. China's state-run media had at one stage reported that the project would form part of a national strategy to divert water from rivers in the south and west to drought-stricken northern areas. The reports said that a 38 million kilowatt power station at Muotuo on the Yarlung Zangbo in Tibet would harness the force of a 9,840 ft drop in terrain over only a few miles.

The capacity of the station would make it the world's largest power generation facility, much bigger than the 18 million kilowatt plant at the Three Gorges. The cost of drilling the tunnel through Mount Namcha Barwa has not yet been announced, but appears likely to surpass £10 billion. At the bottom of the tunnel, the water will flow into a new reservoir and then be diverted along more than 500 miles of the Tibetan Plateau to the vast, arid areas of Xinjiang region and Gansu province. Beijing wants to use large quantities of the plentiful waters of the southwest to top up the Yellow River basin and assuage mounting discontent over water shortages in 600 cities in northern China.

Apprehension has been expressed in some circles that the plans are likely to devastate the lower reaches of the Yarlung Zangbo, which flows south where it becomes the Brahmaputra. This river irrigates the northern plains of Assam state in India before flowing through Bangladesh and emptying into the Bay of Bengal. Lorne Stockman, of the International Tibet Support Group Network, said: "The countries downstream are at the mercy of China in regard to the water flows from the Yarlung Zangbo. During the dry season, the water will be held back to keep the water reservoir full for power generation, and during the monsoon season, the Chinese will be compelled to release the water in bursts."

The new focus on the south and west as a source of energy have caused concern to China's neighbours. Dam projects under way or proposed have prompted protests from countries as far apart as Kazakhstan and Vietnam. In addition to the Brahmaputra river*, development plans on the Tibetan Plateau are set to affect the flow of water out of China into the Mekong, Irrawaddy, Ganges and Indus rivers. ** & ***

---

* **Brahmaputra River**

In the ancient Indian tradition, two rivers are known to originate from Manasarovar Lake, in Mt. Kailash; one flowing to the east is called Brahmaputra and the other flowing to the west was called Shatadru, a tributary of the Sarasvati (joining the latter at Shatrana, Punjab) in Rig Vedic times. Both these major rivers, Brahmaputra and Sarasvati are related to the God of creation, Brahma. Brahmaputra flows about 1800 miles (2900 kms.) from the Kailash range of the Himalayas to join the Ganga River at a vast delta on the Bay of Bengal. It is called the Yarlung Zangbo (also spelled, Tsangpo) in Tibet, the Brahmaputra in Assam and the Jamuna in Bangladesh. Large crafts navigate the river about 800 miles (1290 kms.) upstream. It crosses the Himalayas through gorges 7,150 m (23,458 ft) and 7,756 m

(25,446 ft) deep and then flows south and west-southwest through the Assam Valley in northeastern India, where it is known as the Dihang. During the rainy season there, the river often floods to 8 km wide, rising 9-12 m and depositing sediment carried down from the mountains. The Brahmaputra Valley in Assam has marshy jungle, teak forest, and commercial fisheries; rice, jute, tea, and sugarcane are grown there as well. The river is navigable by steamers and barges for almost 1,300 km to Dibrugarh, India. It joins the Bay of Bengal, in Bangladesh.

** The Tibetan "super dam". Chinese engineers are considering a dam in the Great Yalungzangbo Canyon, the world's deepest, where the river drops 2,340 metres. Installed capacity could be 38,000 megawatts, more than twice that of the Three Gorges, and allow China to influence electricity markets in South Asia. Hamish McDonald Source: Gavan McCormack, 'Water Margins: Competing Paradigms in China', *Critical Asian Studies,* 33:1 (2001). (This story was found at: *http://www.theage.com.au/articles/2003/05/30/1054177725301.html*)

*** Two of the most acute problems China faces today are food and water. These two issues are closely linked and, if not solved, are bound to have grave social and political consequences for the country. A few years ago, Lester Brown, the famous agronomist, advanced a theory: With the growth in China's population (predicted to reach 1.6 billion in 2045) and the increase in industrial development, arable lands reduce rapidly while the needs of population increase simultaneously. With water becoming a rare commodity and agriculture needing more water to sustain production, China has a problem. Moreover, the blue gold is not equally distributed in the Middle Kingdom. Brown's World Watch Institute explains: 'Hydrologically, there are two Chinas—the humid south, which includes the Yangtze River basin and everything south of it, and the north, which includes all the country north of the Yangtze basin. The south, with 700 million people, has one-third of the nation's cropland and four-fifths of its water. The north, with 550 million people, has two-thirds of the cropland and one-fifth of the water. The water per hectare of cropland in the north is one-eighth that of the south.'

The fact that the Chinese government published a White Paper titled 'The Grain Issue in China' shows the issue's vital importance for Beijing's leadership. This led Chinese experts to look around for water. The answer was not far. The Tibetan Plateau is the principal watershed in Asia and the source of its 10 major rivers, including the Brahmaputra (or Yarlung Tsangpo in Tibet), the Sutlej and the Indus. About 90 percent of the Tibetan rivers' runoff flows downstream to China, India, Bangladesh, Nepal, Pakistan, Thailand, Myanmar, Laos, Cambodia and Vietnam. The idea to divert the waters from the south to the north was born.

The scheme has three segments: the eastern, central and western routes. The third is the trickiest; it is the one which should make India and Bangladesh nervous. The southern part of the western route envisages the diversion of the Yarlung Tsangpo, which will have an immense bearing on the lives of millions on the subcontinent. Originating from a glacier near Mount Kailash, it is the largest river on the Tibetan Plateau and the highest on earth. It runs 2,057 kilometers in Tibet before flowing into India, where it becomes the Brahmaputra. One of its interesting characteristics is a sharp U turn (known as the Great Bend) near the Indian border.

It has been discovered recently that the river's gorge forms the longest and deepest canyon in the world. It is in the Great Bend that China is planning one of the most important projects of the diversion scheme. There are two parts: one is the construction of the world's largest hydroelectric plant on the Great Bend dwarfing all other similar projects; the second is the diversion of the waters of the Tsangpo which will be pumped northward across hundreds of kilometers of mountainous region to China's northwestern provinces of Xinjiang and Gansu.

The Tibetans consider the area around the Great Bend, one of the last pristine regions of the world, the home of the Goddess *Dorjee Pagmo*, Tibet's Protecting Deity. They believe this site, locally known as *Pemakö*, is the sacred realm often referred to in their scriptures: a last hidden Shangrila.

The project was first reported in *Scientific American* in June 1996. This article giving credence to the Chinese plans stated: 'Recently some Chinese engineers proposed diverting water into this arid area (*Gobi Desert*) from the mighty Brahmaputra River, which skirts China's southern border before dipping into India and Bangladesh. Such a feat would be impossible with conventional methods, engineers stated at a meeting held last December at the Chinese Academy of Engineering Physics in Beijing. But they added, "we can certainly accomplish this project" with nuclear explosives.'

The *Journal* continued: 'this statement is just one of the many lately in which Chinese technologists and officials have touted the potential of nuclear blasts for carrying out non-military goals.' One of the reasons for China's refusal to ratify the CTBT could be the desire to keep open the option of experimenting with what is called PNE (Peaceful Nuclear Explosion).

In January 1998, the German television channel ZDF presented a feature on Yarlung Tsangpo project in a programme titled *Die Welt* (The World). Its chief planner Professor Chen Chuanyu described the plan to drill a 15 km tunnel through the Himalayas to divert the water before the U turn and direct it to the other end of the bend. This would shorten the approximately 3,000 meters altitude drop, from 200 km to just 15 km. He explained that the hydropower potential could be used to pump water to northwest China over 800 km away.

A complicating aspect was that this area had never been visited by outsiders. The difficult access to this unexplored region must have been one of the greatest obstacles for the engineers in Beijing. At the end of the 1990s, the Chinese government decided to permit foreigners to explore the Grand Canyon. A *National Geographic* expedition, with ultra-sophisticated materials and highly professional rafters, made the first discoveries. The opening of this area to adventure tourism was certainly the first step to find an approach route to the dam site.

Looking first at the dam, India and Bangladesh would be at the mercy of China for adequate release of water during the dry season, and for protection from floods during the rainy season. India knows from its internal problems how difficult it is to solve a water dispute. When it comes to a trans boundary question (where the boundary is not even agreed upon), it would be even more difficult to find a workable solution. Precipitation in north India (particularly Assam) and Bangladesh is very high (80 percent) during the four monsoon months (between June to September) and low (20 percent) during the remaining eight months. China, for her own interests, could withhold water for power generation and irrigation during the dry season and release water during the flood season with catastrophic consequences for eastern South Asia.

The massive diversion of the river to China's northwest could have even more devastating consequences. North India and Bangladesh would be starved of nutrient-rich sediments that enrich the soil of these regions; it would be held back in the reservoir instead of reaching the river's delta. Millions would be affected. A water war could ensue.

The Great Bend is located in a highly earthquake prone area. A huge reservoir and a few PNEs could provoke new earthquakes even more devastating than that in August 1950 when thousands died.

The decision to construct the Lhasa-Golmud line to connect Tibet with China by a railroad has been taken by the Chinese government. The Lhasa-Golmud line is 1,118 kilometres long and a total of 30 bridges need to be built and tunnels dug. The total length of bridges and tunnels is more than 30.6 kilometres and constitutes about 2.7percent of the length of the railway line. The projected total cost of the railway construction based on 1995 price index could amount to a whopping 2.34 billion US$ (19.4 billion Yuan). This would be the first railway line. There are plans to construct three other railway lines connecting Tibet with China. One is the Chengdu-Kongpo-Lhasa route, the other Dali-Kongpo-Lhasa and the third, Lanzhou-Nagchu-Lhasa. There are deep concerns about the effect the railway lines will have on Tibet's fragile ecosystem and their impact on exacerbating erosion, silting and pollution. The military connotation of the railway line could hardly be lost upon India.

When the Chinese embarked on their nuclear programme way back in the 1950s and 1960s they deliberately set up the test sites and nuclear facilities in the remoter parts of China in the west, in Xinjiang and Tibet. The reason was that they wanted them to be as far away as possible from the coast, as both the superpowers of the time had a formidable naval presence in the region. China's fledging navy was no match for them, even just offshore. In addition, it was easier to hide these facilities in the remote regions of China and in the interior of Tibet. The remoteness of the area linked to the sparseness as well as the backwardness of the population ensured that the whereabouts of the complexes and what was going on in them did not leak out. Moreover, in the initial stages, which were the experimental stages for the fabrication of nuclear weapons and delivery systems, enough safeguards were not in place. Therefore, the Chinese were quite happy to push the hazardous effects that might result on to people and regions as far away as possible from the Han heartland. This thinking still obtains, especially as far as Tibet is concerned.

Presently, the Chinese are aiming to achieve superpower status by about 2025, both economically and militarily. Although a nuclear exchange with the other superpower, or for that matter with anyone else would be unthinkable, the military planning for eventualities of this nature is never suspended. The Chinese are alive to the fact that should the USA or another power wish to neutralize China's capability, nuclear weapon sites and missile sites become prime targets. Here again, or so the thinking goes, the neutralization strike by potential adversaries or retaliatory strikes, should they ever take place, would come on to Tibet, a region which has already been despoiled by the Chinese. For the foreseeable future the Chinese mindset is not likely to change. Demilitarization and de-nuclearisation of Tibet can only come about through sustained pressure from the West—the largest trading partners of China being located there.

China has augmented its military modernization budget manifold, both the overt defence budget and that part of the military budget that is hidden from the public gaze. While China pursues its global ambitions in the military and economic spheres, benchmarking these invariably against the US strengths in these fields, countries like India cannot afford to view with equanimity the phenomenal growth of Chinese military potential and forward projections in Tibet and elsewhere around India, regardless of whether a satisfactory boundary agreement with that country is concluded or not.

No consideration of China's military might or its burgeoning military and economic potential whether viewed from New Delhi, Washington, Central Asia or elsewhere can overlook the transfer of lethal military hardware, which includes transfers in the nuclear and missile technology fields to Pakistan. Up to the unfolding of the September 11 events, these transfers, although disturbing were generally viewed in the other world capitals as problem areas for India or the non-proliferation regimes that supposedly had come into force. Post-September 11, 2001 the larger and more horrifying dimensions of these transfers became apparent; most notably, the possibility of re-transfer of these lethal technologies via Pakistan to entities that avowedly intended to introduce WMD into their terror networks. China being one of Pakistan's closest allies and backers in the military field could not have been unaware of the transfers that could have been, or were, in the pipeline from the Pakistan military-cum-ISI hierarchy to the Taliban and Osama bin Laden.

The Chinese on the one hand were strengthening their agreements with the Central Asian Republics and Russia as part of the Shanghai Co-operation Organization [SCO]. At the same time, they had started interacting with the Taliban, possibly to secure their own flank in Xinjiang against the spread of Islamic jehad organizations. Giving the benefit of the doubt to China the conclusion, nevertheless, becomes inescapable that China was at no stage unaware of the Taliban/bin Laden push into Central Asia through Islamic jehad activities that were professedly bent upon overthrowing the Central Asian regimes with whom China was ostensibly cementing its relationship at a different level. They could not have been unaware of the fact that the Taliban/bin Laden/ISI elements were fomenting trouble against their strategic partner Russia. Throughout, the Chinese were aware of the cross border terrorism that was taking place in Kashmir, often with Chinese weapons.

Many people—outside Pakistan and Afghanistan—had started becoming apprehensive at the type of technology transfers that China was making to its Pakistani allies. It was consciously abetting the strengthening of the Pakistan nuclear arsenal and the delivery systems, notably the longer-range missiles. It had made overtures to the Taliban from the outset, possibly to build bridges with the new order taking shape in Afghanistan and perhaps to limit the help being extended to the Uighur separatist elements in Xinjiang. There had been disturbing reports appearing from time to time of increasing economic and security ties between China and the Taliban. Most people did not discount them because it appeared to be a natural extension of help being extended by China to Taliban's creators, the Pakistan military and the ISI. Deeper linkages could have been in the offing between Beijing, Islamabad, Kabul, and on to Central Asia, following in the wake of the Taliban's northward thrust. It is not entirely dissimilar to what the US is now attempting to do from another direction—Washington, London, Islamabad, Kabul, Tashkent and on to the rest of Central Asia. Russia is poised delicately between these two geo-strategic thrust lines, one from the East and the other from the West. The first one temporarily suppressed, possibly going into a state of dormancy, the latter in its hyperactive stage. India, Iran and Russia could play a moderating role to roll back both these extra-territorial urges, to provide breathing space to Central Asia and, at a later stage to Afghanistan, Pakistan and the rest of South Asia.

Immediately after the September 11 attacks, China, like the rest of the world, supported US initiatives to fight global terrorism. There was not much ambiguity in the quickness or quality of the response. Doubtless, the Chinese would have let it be known that USA would be expected to tone down its rhetoric and support for Taiwan and Tibet. However, as the Anglo-American designs for post-Taliban strategies in Central Asia started to become clearer China had second thoughts on the subject.

## Promising Developments

Infrequently, enlightened policies, but more frequently altered ground realities 'oblige' nations to change course, often dramatically. That is what could be happening to relations between China and India. Essentially, cause and effect: Pakistan, the 'all-weather friend' of China, the constant ally of the West in its fight against communism, decided upon the demise of the Soviet Union to flex its muscles in its backyard (Afghanistan). It brought the Americans to China's backyard in a manner that could scarcely have been conceived by the latter. For the big players of Asia—China, Russia and India—the impressive US presence represents a geopolitical upheaval of an order of magnitude. China and Russia can only view the presence in their underbelly with trepidation. Of the three, currently India feels the least threatened. This is the backdrop against which a historic *rapprochement* between the two Asian giants might be in the offing. It could be sustained if lingering doubts on both sides are simultaneously addressed following the visit to China of the Indian Prime Minister, Atal Behari Vajpayee in June 2003. Indian worries include: China's rising military spending; ongoing attempts at encirclement; continuing transfer of dangerous technologies to Pakistan; the prolonged repression in Tibet along with ethnic swamping and deculturisation that continue apace. On China's part it would suspect that: while the government of India may keep yielding ground on Tibet, it remains an emotive issue for most Indians and Tibetans and the government's actions may not be reflective of the sentiments of the people; India already has unshakeably strong ties with Russia and Vietnam, it could soon develop much stronger ties with Japan, Taiwan, South Korea and the Central Asian Republics; unless locked into a very solid relationship with China in the coming years, India might be tempted to succumb to US blandishments. Casting aside mutual suspicion, China and India can revert to the era of friendship and harmony that marked their relations over several millennia.

However, irreversibility in the positive direction can realistically be maintained only if China follows up on the recent accords by reaching an accommodation with the Dalai Lama and both countries proceed thereafter with the gradual demilitarization of Tibet and the contiguous Himalayan region. A bold step of such magnitude could then become the harbinger of a millennium of peace for these two nations and possibly for Asia and the world as well.

## SUBCONTINENTAL INSECURITIES

The military reality on the subcontinent in the first half of the opening decade of the Twenty-first century is that Pakistan is partially under occupation by the US forces: in some respects physically; and in others more subtly. The situation in Afghanistan while somewhat similar has many variations whose outcome remains uncertain. India has ceded place to the US as the prime mover and guarantor for the restoration of peace in India's neighbourhood: in different degrees in Sri Lanka, Nepal, Pakistan, Afghanistan and Bangladesh.

### India

For full 50 years and more India has been led by the nose by Pakistan, in a manner of speaking, both internally and externally. India's policy has almost invariably been reactive. No doubt Bangladesh was an outstanding success. However, the military gains were fast dissipated in Pakistan as well as in Bangladesh post-1971. Irrespective of the decline of

Pakistan itself on the global arena in recent years, it is undeniable that Pakistan succeeded brilliantly in the following domains:

- Undermined India's efforts at securing a permanent seat in the UN Security Council.
- Keeping the Kashmir question alive in global forums.
- In concert with China limiting India's access to Central Asia.
- Reducing the colossus called India into a whimpering giant by forcing it to *plead* before the world community to save it from cross border terrorism emanating from Pakistan.
- Putting India on the defensive on several counts.
- Forcing India to expend enormous outlays to counter the threat of low intensity conflict generated by Pakistan or sponsored by Pakistan.
- Creating adverse situations on the Indo-Nepal and Indo-Bangladesh borders.
- In concert with Saudi Arabia contributing to the enormous proliferation of *madrasas* in India and other parts of the subcontinent, notably Bangladesh and the Indo-Nepal border.
- Sustaining militant groups in the northeast in spite of the crushing military defeat in East Bengal in 1971.
- Multiplication of jehadi cells in many parts of India and the subcontinent.
- Circulation of large amounts of fake currency in the country.
- In concert with its sympathizers in Bangladesh forcing an exodus of Hindus from that country.
- Pushing in hostile elements for permanent residence in India for carrying out anti-India activities at opportune moments.

- Domination of the underworld in Mumbai and other areas on the West Coast through its proxies based in Mumbai.
- Infiltration of the Mumbai film industry.
- Furthering political–criminal nexus in many of the western states notably, Maharastra and Gujarat.
- Militancy in J&K.
- Innumerable acts of subversion, sabotage and terrorism.
- Subversion of the Muslim psyche and setting up of pan-Islamic movements with anti-India overtones.

When looked at dispassionately the implications of the tabulations made above should have a sobering effect. It is inconceivable that a country the size of India with resources that far outmatch its adversary, Pakistan should have allowed this state of affairs to continue for decades on end. This in spite of having got the better of Pakistan in four wars against that country. Had an adverse situation developed for India in any of the conflicts the consequences for India would have been far too grim to even think about. Therefore, the question to be addressed is whether India is intrinsically weak or whether it has been artificially weakened through wrong policies, wrong military priorities and an inability to grasp the essentials of the threat that it faces from Pakistan and the manner in which it should be handled. Some of the anomalies that had crept into the thinking had resulted from, *inter alia,* looking at Pakistan in 'isolation', even after it had become abundantly clear to the defence planners of India that China's and Western, now US, support to Pakistan was essential in underpinning the defensive viability of the latter.

For India to emerge as an important player on the global scene, it has to be able to tackle the radical Islamist threat from Pakistan adequately in the shortest possible time frame, without resorting to full-scale war. Unless it does so and demonstrates its capacity to do so, it cannot expect to be taken seriously by the rest of the world as a strong presence on the international arena. Therefore, unless India has a viable capacity for breaking the impasse that has developed on the subject of cross border terrorism it would not be in a position to prevent the rise of Muslim fundamentalism on the subcontinent. It needs to be mentioned here that by and large India's approach to the threat from Pakistan, which does not seem to be diminishing in spite of huge outlays on defence vis-à-vis Pakistan, has invariably been a reaction to the actions taken by Pakistan in as far as it relates to the activities of the armed forces of India and the intelligence fraternity. Therefore, unless new avenues for dealing with the Pakistan military are explored—and exploited—the chances of arriving at a *modus vivendi* with Pakistan, suitable for India, will be remote.

The Government of India has come in for considerable criticism, both from outside the country and within at the handling of Pakistan over the years. What many people find inexplicable is that a country the size of India should continue to plead to other countries that they should restrain Pakistan, which intrinsically can be no match for India seeing their relative strengths. Hence, the fault for India's supposed helplessness in dealing effectively with Pakistan must lie in wrong prioritization of force structuring and weapons acquisitions, as also the fixation on an unproductive one-track defence strategy, which ignored several other options available to the country to put Pakistan in its place.

In the earlier decades India could not take advantage of its victories over Pakistan in spite of its obvious superiority because military analysts tended to look at the Pakistan military in isolation; whereas Pakistani military capabilities can only be understood in the light of its relationships with many other countries that have sustained and bolstered the Pakistani state through support to the Pakistan military. This pitfall has to be avoided in the emerging circumstances. Pakistani strength has to be viewed holistically as part of the grand design of the Pakistani army as also the interests that it has served of other nations interested in, or interfering in the affairs of the subcontinent. A departure can be made by analyzing the whole gamut of Pakistani affairs, especially after the takeover by General Musharraf and the happenings of 9/11. Not only the Pakistan army, the Pakistan state itself has been subjected to massive turbulence in the last 5 years. The depth and extent of the turbulence have been described in the book *Restructuring Pakistan*[4]. However, what needs to be reiterated is the fact that over several decades while assessing the strength and weakness of the Pakistan army emphasis was invariably placed solely on relative military strengths of the two sides. It can be shown that although India will have to maintain overwhelming military strength in the coming years for warding off challenges that relate more to China's growing strength rather than that of Pakistan, defeating or diluting the strength of the Pakistan army in purely conventional military terms is no longer feasible, unless Pakistan is foolhardy enough to undertake military strikes or types of provocation for which full-scale war would remain the only option. Cross border terrorism does not fall into these categories.

Because of its internal contradictions and the policies followed by the Pakistan army after the takeover by Pervez Musharraf, either of its own volition or due to US pressure, these have led to the development of fault lines. Properly analysed and understood these would indicate the extent to which the Pakistan army and, by extension, the very existence of the Pakistani state in its present form is being compromised. In most cases, India simply has to closely watch and monitor the situation. It is not required to do very much by way of overt actions in Pakistani territory. The tensions brought on by the actions of the Pakistan army will automatically lead to its weakening and possibly wholesale decline. In most fields, where the fissures between the Pakistan army and its opponents are rapidly expanding the hands off policy would be in India's best interest.

There is no doubt that the threat to Indian security today is greatest from global terrorism, linked to Islamic fundamentalism. It is amenable to instigation, support or training from Pakistan. This kind of threat is all-pervasive and can surface from within the country or from the west or the east, as is being witnessed with increasing frequency via Bangladesh and even Nepal, putting the entire northeast in danger. It is not so much the potency of the threat as it exists today, but its alarming potential due to the inability of the governments of India to take decisive and what is more timely action.

## Pakistan

The situation for Pakistan as well has changed dramatically in recent years. Earlier projections relating to Pakistan, especially after the 1971 war with that country suffered from a major drawback in that Pakistan's strength was looked at in a stand alone fashion. Whereas, by hindsight, it would be apparent to most defence analysts that Pakistan derives a large portion of its strength from its external relationships, especially its close ties with USA, China, Saudi Arabia and many other Muslim countries, based on religion. Because of the continued US backing over several decades, many Western powers, Japan and other close US allies also helped Pakistan along in different ways. Post-9/11 some of these relationships may have changed. Whatever its ability—or strength—to undermine India internally and from across India's borders on the subcontinent, Pakistan as a state stands diminished due to the physical occupation of bases in Pakistan and Afghanistan by outside forces. Not only do they have a free run within the bases that they occupy, they can foray outwards from time to time, with or without Pakistani consent or assistance. Therefore, in evaluating the strength of the Pakistani armed forces, especially its army, which has ruled the roost for most of its history, the outcome of the struggle in Afghanistan becomes a critical factor.

Taken together all these factors present an interesting picture. The holistic appraisal that becomes possible thereby provides insights, which become sharper only when looked at against the larger backdrop. In isolation they may not present a similar picture. Together they indicate that if the present policies adopted by Pakistan continue in the direction that they have been moving due to the need of the military dictator to retain hold on power and the Pakistan army to remain in the ascendant, the collapse of the Pakistani state could come about in time frames spanning a few years or at best one or two decades.

Pakistan's present difficulties, as in the case of many other developing countries, stem from neglect of the social sector over a long period of time. Pakistan's defence expenditure as percentage of total expenditure has been hovering around twenty five percent since about 1980. Paradoxically, in spite of the reduction of the external threat (after the Soviet withdrawal from Afghanistan), Pakistan's sense of insecurity actually deepened. Drug trafficking, increasing societal violence, terrorism and sectarianism linked to the spread of small arms all contribute to the insecurity. There is an awareness that the superior firepower of the Pakistan army might not count for very much for stemming the onslaught of motivated jehadi fighters in urban surroundings should they cross and re-cross in ever larger numbers from Afghanistan to Pakistan and back – as they seem to be doing—for helping their counterparts in Pakistan. By pushing itself to the forefront during the formative stages of the movement for introduction of radical Islam into Pakistani society, the Pakistan military did not anticipate the quagmire into which it was plunging when it assumed the responsibility of becoming the guardian of the Islamic ideological identity. In this exercise it tried to displace even the Mullahs; now the Mullahs are attempting to displace the military. In the initial stages the exercise was undertaken more from the point of view of strengthening the military's position vis-à-vis the political dispensation than from any special leaning toward Islamic purity. The difference being that after having continued the pretence for nearly twenty years the Pakistan military has virtually cut off its escape routes.

The attention of the world is suddenly focused on Pakistan, not as the people of Pakistan have been led to believe as a frontline state for the ' Battle of Afghanistan', but as a prelude to the 'Battle for Pakistan' that must surely follow, at whatever stage after a degree of stabilisation in Afghanistan and Iraq. The US–led coalition may not at the moment feel that the situation might be as grim as in Afghanistan. It would yet be mindful of recent history in this regard—i.e., the sudden collapse of the USSR, the fall of the Berlin Wall, the fall of Saigon and the return of the Ayatollah to Iran.

Since Pakistan has centred its existence around confrontation with India, it would follow that any increase in India's economic strength and ability to deal with the low intensity conflict and cross-border terrorism sponsored by Pakistan will impact heavily on Pakistan's internal condition.* China, while continuing to back Pakistan could have misgivings after the US intervention. Its support, though seemingly enduring, will itself be contingent upon the progress of the US intervention in Afghanistan, Iraq, Pakistan and Central Asia. The strengthening of Indo-US relations could be further influenced as much by China's geopolitical strategy in Asia and the transfer of nuclear materials and missile technologies; which are likely to be viewed far more seriously in the future than was the case in the earlier decade.

---

* The Pakistan establishment has been so intimately involved with the terrorist organizations nurtured by them for so long that disengagement, even it were to be finally mandated by the military top brass would be difficult, if not impossible. During an interview given to a news channel, Star TV in early 2002 on the heels of the press conference by the then Indian army chief, this author had stated *inter alia* that while it might be true that through its proxy war or Low Intensity Conflict Pakistan was pursuing its strategy of bleeding the Indian army by a thousand cuts, seeing the size of India and the Indian army these were all flesh wounds to which salve could be applied, in the process Pakistan was haemorrhaging internally, a potentially fatal condition. Schisms have further developed amongst the terrorist organizations based in Pakistan between those that continue to enjoy support from Pakistan's ISI and those considered beyond the pale. However, quite a few of the prominent terrorist groups that are close to or remain substantially controlled by the ISI have large number of cadres deeply sympathetic to Al-Qaeda and its affiliates, regardless of their leadership's perceived closeness with their military and ISI handlers. These elements have been suspected of moonlighting for the more radical groups opposed to the policies of the military regime.

In the light of the foregoing, the author in a BBC interview in London on 16 September 2003 had questioned the wisdom of the Western world putting all its eggs in the basket of the military dictator of Pakistan.

It would hardly be an exaggeration to state that the Pakistani generals have ended up by making their region a war zone. Forces from many parts of the world will gather here to decide amongst themselves the future of Afghanistan and quite possibly Pakistan. The generals have become pawns in a game which they started but did not know how to end. It ended by blowing up in their face. When and if the foreigners leave, nobody knows; certainly not the people of Pakistan or the Pakistani generals. All decisions will be taken in Washington and not Islamabad. Not even in New Delhi. The generals still do not talk of a return to democracy. They want to use Afghanistan's—and Pakistan's—misfortune to strengthen their hold.

## Afghanistan

The problems for the Americans in Afghanistan could result more from the latent potential of the Taliban to re-emerge in Pakistan, or elsewhere on the subcontinent, at a later date with a view to renewing their activities. As part of the US strategy many local commanders who supported the Taliban were induced to change sides or to distance themselves from the Taliban. This strategy could work in the short run. It could create problems at a later date. Tribal leaders who are buyable can just as easily be repurchased by others, should the price be right. Hence, to base post-intervention governance strategy for Afghanistan on the shifting sands of purchased loyalty might not turn out to be a sound proposition.

Over two years after the US intervention in Afghanistan and the euphoria generated by the early success in routing of the Taliban regime in Kabul the situation in Afghanistan no longer looks as rosy. Anxiety is mounting as reports keep coming in of the regrouping of the Taliban-Al Qaeda cadres in Pakistan with the tacit support of the radical groups there as well as the continuing support from elements in the

Pakistan military and ISI who have been traditional supporters of the Taliban. As if these reports were not enough cause for concern alternate channels have apparently been established for the continuous flow of funds to groups who are avowedly bent upon exacting their revenge upon America and the Americans, wherever they happen to be. Unless dealt with efficaciously in the near future it is possible that the revitalized jehadi groups could emerge stronger than heretofore with a larger and deeper base in Pakistan, especially in the tribal areas of NWFP, Baluchistan and parts of Afghanistan that constituted the traditional support base of the Taliban.

These developments tend to reinforce the view that the situation in the erstwhile Afghanistan-Pakistan cauldron that became the bedrock for the most virulent form of global terrorism cannot be viewed in isolation. Without some restructuring in Pakistan a resolution of the Afghanistan problem would be problematic. The following indicators of developments within Afghanistan need to be assessed:

- Russia would continue to ensure that its new defence line for the containment of Islamic *jehad* rests along the Hindukush and not in the Central Asian Republics or in the Russian Republics with predominant Muslim majorities.
- Iran and Uzbekistan would continue their efforts to carve out respective spheres of influence in the northwest and north.
- Pakistan is unlikely to stop interfering in the developments in Afghanistan unless it is obliged to do so. This support from Pakistan – overt or covert— remains the single biggest factor militating against the unification of Afghanistan. Were it to become possible to exclude support from Pakistan to the radical elements – an extremely difficult proposition at the present juncture – a measure of stability could return to Afghanistan.

- China while part of the global alliance against terrorism would in all probability continue its support to the Pakistan military regime to enable it to withstand US pressure; not because China is against the global effort to contain Islamic jehad, but because it cannot view continued US presence in the region with any degree of comfort.
- In spite of the inroads made by the US to increase its influence in the Central Asian Republics, Russia and USA are likely to continue to remain on the same side in the fight against global terrorism. Oil politics for the outflow of hydrocarbon reserves from Central Asia is an entirely different issue where existing divides could deepen.
- For the foreseeable future Indian perspectives remain in conformity with those of the US and UN for the restoration of stability in Afghanistan.

## Demographic Dynamic

A major causative factor for the increasing non-governability of Pakistan – to some extent other countries of the subcontinent as well—is the horrendous population growth and the concomitant destruction of the natural environment. This, in itself, becomes sufficient cause for societal violence and the spread of small arms. For, had the population of the subcontinent, which was around eight hundred million plus at the beginning of the nineteen eighties decade, stabilised at around that figure or even at a slightly higher level, many of the intractable problems that these nations face today, especially increased societal violence, would not have been there, or even if they had manifested themselves they would not have seemed intractable. The corollary to this statement would also hold good. Should Pakistan's population double in the next twenty-five to thirty years, as it is bound to do at the present growth rate, governing Pakistan could become a near impossibility, irrespective of the form of government in place.

Today the subcontinent has reached a stage of overpopulation that should it become technically feasible to project ten thousand people every day to a colony on the moon or Mars it would not make a dent in the population growth rate or lead to an improvement in livability in most parts. Cities bursting at the seams with the deprived segments still continuing to proliferate is a dimension of the problem that has not received sufficient attention in Pakistan or a purposeful move towards its tackling. It is leading to a lowered quality of life for the majority of the inhabitants and results in further breakdown of the social cohesion of society. If it remains unchecked it will lead to greater societal violence and sectarian conflicts as the resource base shrinks. The need to kill the others will no longer be met by the simpler variety of small arms being used today in Karachi and elsewhere in Pakistan.

## Renewed Manifestations of Terror

The ISI-Al Qaeda-Taliban triumvirate showed the way on September 11, 2001. It was the first time. It is unlikely to be the last. The American administration has made it clear that the collapse of the Taliban regime in Afghanistan does not mean the end of war against terrorism. The Taliban provided the focus and locus for the initial phase of America's counteraction against global terrorism. With the disintegration of the Taliban, USA was able to send a message that states supporting terrorism would be dealt with severely.

Several other issues, mostly socio-economic in nature, impinge on South Asian stability and harmony. Of necessity, these have to form part of a more comprehensive formulation. But more than anything else it is the nature of the conflict that was brought upon by the events of September 11, that has overwhelmed the military dimension of South Asian security. Once the pattern of the intervention of the US-led coalition in the Afghan-Pakistan region was established, most if not all outcomes in the foreseeable future not only in South Asia, but in the adjoining region as well, would be contingent upon the outcome of the intervention itself and the direction that Pakistan takes in the form of governance that is eventually established in that country. For the time being India is watching from the sidelines, planning and activating its own response against cross-border terrorism. Should, however, the situation in Pakistan worsen to the point of intractability India may have to play a bigger role in concert with many other principal actors of the global community to ensure that the pent up militant zeal of the religious orthodoxy does not again become the bedrock for renewed global terror.

## End Notes

1. *The Statesman,* 19 June 2002.
2. *New Scientist,* 1 March 2003.
3. See also *AAMAR ASOM* 21 July 2003, 'Alarm to the State: China will stop the "Luit" (Brahmaputra) in Tibet' by Digjyoti Lahkar and 'China to Conduct Feasibility Study on Hydropower Project in Tibet', *People's Daily,* 17 July 2003.
4. Vinod Saighal, *Restructuring Pakistan,* New Delhi: Manas Publications, 2002.

# 2

## China, Tibet, India: Status Quo or Reappraisal?

China and India represent two of the earliest civilizations that have been able to continuously hold on to their traditions since the dawn of history.[1] Historically, China has had a tradition of world dominance through power projections (i.e. The Middle Kingdom ideation). India, on the other hand, has never aspired to military or economic dominance. In ancient times, when India was a powerful country, the only influence it projected was that of peace and tranquility. Moving on from that earlier period it would be interesting to look at the growth patterns adopted by the two countries since regaining their freedom after the Second World War. China fought its way to freedom. India, having taken recourse to Gandhian pacifism, had freedom delivered to it. There was, however, an enormous price tag attached to the pacific route to freedom—the violent partition of the country. After establishment of Chinese unity through the bloody route, the Chinese leaders understood, more comprehensively than anyone else, that power, in the ultimate analysis, did flow from the barrel of a gun. Having understood the currency of power they quickly went on to occupy Tibet while India was embroiled in Kashmir. Indian leaders were not able to grasp the global reality of that period. They tried to rebuild India on the platform of idealism. They made way for the Chinese in Tibet. They have been making way for the Chinese ever since.

The China, Tibet, India (CTI) region stretches from the Pacific rim to the Indian Ocean. The landmass is immense, the population of the two giants that bestride the sparsely populated country in the middle no less so. From that sparsely populated country between China and India debouch river systems that cover over 40 percent of the world's population. Seeing the overwhelming dependence of practically half the world's population on the ecological well-being of the Tibetan Plateau, its demilitarization is now an ecological imperative, which does not brook further delay. Continued militarisation of the Tibetan Plateau, along with the attendant militarisation of the eastern Himalayas as a direct consequence thereof, would not only affect the indigenous Tibetan population, but entire communities from the Indus to the Yellow River.

Militarisation of any region takes place on account of perceived military threats to that region. In the second half of the twentieth century the Chinese rapidly militarised Tibet to consolidate their grip on the conquered territory. In addition to the internal unrest caused by the occupation they might have had misgivings regarding the intentions of India and/or the USA. Mention is made of only these two countries because no other nation or community of nations had, or would be likely to have in the foreseeable future, the direct interest or the military wherewithal to mount any credible challenge to continued Chinese occupation of Tibet. Today the world at large and certainly USA and India are reconciled to the Chinese presence in Tibet. The misgivings that China may have entertained in the twentieth century—if at all—of being militarily challenged in Tibet cannot obtain at the dawn of the twenty-first century. Therefore, since no country seriously questions the status quo, China can safely undertake the demilitarisation of the Tibetan Plateau and the loosening of its harsh grip on the Tibetan people without any qualms. The perceived *raison d'etre* for the militarisation of Tibet having disappeared altogether in the new millennium makes it possible for the Chinese to arrive at an accommodation with the Dalai Lama and undertake demilitarisation without a backward glance.

## China, Tibet, India – the 20th Century Relationships

Today, the view from Beijing on the Tibetan issue would be that everything is moving along better than expected. From the Chinese standpoint it is a dead issue. Washington and the European capitals, they feel, keep the issue alive merely to embarrass China. In the Chinese perception, as far as the West is concerned economics will, hereafter, propel geopolitics. Hence, if geo-economics is what matters China is exceptionally well placed – at least for the time being. The other power that has any locus standi is India. As Beijing sees it, India does not have the stomach to question China's policy in Tibet. Should it ever develop the urge to speak out, China can always use Pakistan and the Kashmir card to put paid to India's boldness. Therefore, by themselves the Dalai Lama and the Tibetans in exile numbering a 100,000 plus count for almost nothing in the Chinese reckoning at the beginning of the twenty-first century. Whatever residual interest the world may manifest from time to time on this question, it is an interest that is on the wane. The UN would not like to get involved in Tibet either, China being a permanent member of the Security Council, with the veto right.

In the light of the foregoing, whichever way the issue is looked at from Beijing, the Government of China sees no advantage in settling the Tibet issue. Talking to the Dalai

Lama is a mere sop. China holds all the cards, the Tibetans, after 50 years, almost none, other than the persona of the Dalai Lama. Nor, for that matter does the Government of India at this point in time. The question then arises, "can China be induced to talk seriously to the Dalai Lama or his representatives on the question of Tibetan autonomy"? China has apparently concluded it has nothing to gain. Even if serious talks are held, these could drag on for decades – like the boundary question with India – while the de-culturisation of Tibet continues.

China is seen by the world as the second power of the globe today. It is fast becoming an economic giant. Its military capability is improving day by day. Practically the whole of Tibet lies prostrate. In the outer provinces that have been more comprehensively assimilated the younger generation in the cities speaks Chinese. In another twenty years, the old Tibetan culture would be a fading memory. Such may not be the case as yet in TAR, outside the big cities. However, even in Tibet Autonomous Region (TAR) the Tibetan population is being gradually assimilated with the Chinese mainland. Economic assimilation brings its rewards for the younger generation. The process will be completed within this decade, or the next, once the Lhasa Railway is pushed further westwards from the mainland into Tibet. At that stage, in the second decade of the 21st century, or later, whenever the Dalai Lama leaves the world stage, the Tibetan diaspora itself could lose its relevance for the people of Tibet and possibly for the world outside India.

Global forces also seem to be militating against Tibet, and in some ways—albeit unintentionally—helping China. The first and foremost of these is the process of globalisation based on the American model of market capitalism and heightened consumerism. Heightened consumerism being another form of excessive self-indulgence generates among its adherents, whose number with each passing year is growing exponentially, increased lust, greed, anger, impatience and the urge to get rich quick, regardless of the consequences to their homelands, to the earth or to themselves. The older generation may still mourn the passing of the older ways, the younger generation has no such nostalgia. They do not look to the past. They look to the future. That future has been spelt out for the Tibetan youth in Lhasa, Shigatse and elsewhere by the Chinese in dazzling letters, which read, 'to be rich is glorious'; 'follow us and we will make you rich'; 'get rich quick and enjoy yourself, nothing else matters'.

It is the new face of China. It is the new face of Tibet and the Tibetan exiles, especially amongst the youth looking for a ticket to USA and the West. It is the new face of the young Indians in metropolitan cities. It is the new face of the younger generation practically throughout the world. It is leading to alienation. It is leading to de-culturisation. It is leading to a turning away from the past. Whatever anyone might say, in this endeavour the Chinese, the Americans and the West appear to be on the same side, the Tibetan question and the regional or global geopolitics notwithstanding.

The theme of the demilitarisation of the Tibetan Plateau should not, hereafter, be tackled solely from the political plane, where it remained intractable for over four decades. The issue should now be tackled on a plane where no system, political entity or group need feel alienated or excluded from the process. It would then become possible to rationalise the type of exchanges (between China and India) that could lead to an enlarged Tibetan cultural space as a prelude to the demilitarisation of the Tibetan Plateau and the return of the Dalai Lama and his people. These could encompass inter alia:

- Demilitarisation of the Himalayas;
- India-China geo-strategic realignment;

- Sino-Indian cultural rapprochement;
- Spiritual renaissance in China, especially the rural areas;
- A manifold increase in trade between the two countries.

## Peering into the Future

China's latest plans to construct the proposed Lhasa-Golmud Railway line could mean that more Chinese settlers would be able to swamp Tibet; and Tibet's untapped natural resources would find their way to China. Within a decade of the coming up of the railway, Tibet itself could presumably go the way of Inner Mongolia and Manchuria—totally swamped by Chinese settlers and completely sinicised. Many people feel that the decision to construct the line connecting central Tibet with China is a political decision, which has strong political and military overtones. Evidently, the coming up of the railway line, despite objections about the un-sustainability of the project, will have a major bearing on India's security as it would increase manifold the Chinese ability to move troops and supplies rapidly across the vast Tibetan Plateau.

Looking into the future one of the first aspects that springs to mind is that the China, Tibet, India equation of the twentieth century has not carried over into the 21st in the manner that it developed over the last fifty years. Many climactic changes have since taken place that could alter significantly the dynamics of the equation between the three countries or two countries and one occupied entity, which, no matter the degree of demographic swamping, repression or forced absorption that takes place, will always retain its distinctiveness in the eyes of the world. Before the dawn of the new century and especially before the events of 11 September 2001, China could have unilaterally furthered any of its designs vis-à-vis Tibet without India or the world being able to do anything about it. Today, the situation stands altered. It is not as if India has developed the ability or the desire to intervene physically in Tibet or that the rest of the world is about to challenge, after fifty years, China's occupation of Tibet. It is only that China's ability to visit the type of horrors perpetrated earlier on the Tibetans will no longer go unchallenged. Certain currents could develop that might make China recoil in a manner that may not have been possible in the last fifty years.

The changes that have taken place that might make enlightened elements in China realize that further erosion of the Tibetan culture or suppression of the Tibetan people might prove counterproductive can be tabulated as:

- The physical US presence in areas contiguous to China in Central Asia, Afghanistan and even Pakistan; the presence is of a nature that would allow it to monitor almost every missile launch activity directly from ranges that are so close as to abort the launch at the take-off or launch stage itself, thereby crippling China's offensive capability to a considerable degree;
- USA's increasing ability to ring China with theatre missile defences from many directions;
- India's ability a few years down the line to counter China's nuclear one-sidedness that existed practically throughout the last fifty years;
- India's growing self-assurance in its foreign policy formulations;
- The dramatic improvement in India's economic condition compared to what it was merely ten or twelve years ago;

- The physical US presence in Pakistan might impair China's ability in the future to tie down India in a South Asian quagmire that China to an extent helped create by transferring nuclear and missile technology to its client state;
- India's growing ability to help in the stability of Central Asia.

For several decades India was a little more than a bit player vis-à-vis China in Central or South East Asia or for that matter anywhere else, with some exceptions. Therefore, it really did not have many options regarding Tibet. Not only did it supinely accept Chinese outrages in Tibet, linked to developments that threatened the security of India, it curtailed severely the options that could have been exercised by the Dalai Lama to enlarge the Tibetan question. It needs to be restated here that India did not advocate the challenging of China's position in Tibet in the last century, nor does it wish to do so now, unless China by its actions forces India and the rest of the world to throw open the whole question of the occupation of Tibet. To obviate such a situation the obvious course for China would be to settle the boundary dispute with India and meet the very reasonable minimum demands of the Dalai Lama.

China has sat on the question of autonomy for Tibetans and the boundary dispute with India for several decades. It may not be prudent for it to prolong these issues in the fashion that it did before. Dramatic changes could take place that might not be in China's interest if it continues to drag its feet from a position of near-absolute unassailability, to the extent that the world had practically reconciled itself to the Chinese position, primarily because the prime contenders, India and the Dalai Lama, were not willing to challenge it or do anything about it. The world would now expect China to, at the very least, adhere to the following norms while it drags out the negotiations with the Dalai Lama:

- Immediate stop to further demographic swamping of Tibet by Han settlers;
- Prepare a programme for phased pullback of the Han settlers brought in earlier;
- Cessation of repression of the Tibetan people;
- Full autonomy to the Dalai Lama and his representatives to take over and revitalise all Tibetan monasteries;
- Immediate halt to the ecological devastation of Tibet;
- Participate in the global programme for the ecological restoration of Tibet in concert with the representatives of the Dalai Lama.

## The Way Forward

The Dalai Lama remains deeply committed to the Gandhian philosophy of non-violence. He has given Gandhi's concept a new dimension. The Tibetan struggle that he leads does not call for the oppressor to quit his land. He is willing to adjust to the reality of the situation. He would be satisfied with Tibetan autonomy. One reason why the Chinese fear a direct dialogue with the Dalai Lama is that they would not like to thereby expose the Chinese public to his persona, whom they have so persistently reviled. They are not even sure what their own reaction would be. They have been watching with unease country after country succumbing to his charm. Unarguably—whether the concerned people agree with his political formulations or otherwise—there would hardly be anybody who when face to face with the Dalai Lama would be able to sustain a personal animus against him. His laughter is infectious, his warmth all-embracing, his simplicity endearing. That would perhaps explain the persistent hostility that the Chinese continue to maintain towards him. It is they—the mighty power—who feel insecure. Not him.

The fourteenth Dalai Lama started out as a leader of the Tibetans, as the repository of their hopes and aspirations, for this world and the next. The intervening decades have seen his stature grow to that of a world leader, who remains in the forefront of humanity's march towards a more humane world order. His cause is no longer just the cause of the preservation of a unique culture of a few million Tibetans. The successful outcome of the epic struggle of this Buddhist sage and his people will be an important landmark for the human race in its quest for universal brotherhood. Surprisingly, and perhaps not unsurprisingly, the biggest beneficiaries will be the Chinese themselves.

The world has been so inured to the China, Tibet, India equation of the previous century that it failed to take into account the importance of perhaps one of the most significant developments of recent years as it moved into the new century. The epoch-making event that needs to be emblazoned across all points of the horizon is that in spite of the merciless repression visited upon the fragile Tibetan nation—fragile in numbers and fragile in its ecology—since the Chinese invaded Tibet the Dalai Lama has remained steadfast in his belief in non-violence. Any other leader, recoiling in horror at the magnitude of the devastation wrought on Tibet and its people, would long ago have changed course; in the manner of so many insurgent and terrorist organizations that have sprung up all over the world to cause a veritable nightmare for the well-being of so many nations. The Dalai Lama stood rock-like in his belief in *ahimsa* as propounded by the Buddha several millennia ago and as practiced by Mahatma Gandhi in the 20$^{th}$ century when challenging the might of the greatest empire of that age. The Dalai Lama's steadfastness becomes doubly commendable in the face of the bitter opposition by a large portion of the Tibetan youth who do not see any hope for salvation—for their country or people—at the other end of the road taken by their spiritual leader, no matter how much they might revere him personally.

This self-sacrifice and steadfastness of the Tibetan people to uphold the values they cherish, in the face of prolonged inhuman repression has to be seen in contrast to the violence and suicide bombings erupting elsewhere in the world in the face of much lesser wrongs, imagined or real, perpetrated against oppressed people. Today it is perhaps the only experiment of its type on a large enough scale that the world is aware of. It cannot be allowed to fail. More, so for the sake of humanity at large than just the Tibetan people. The whole world has an immense stake in seeing the Dalai Lama's experiment succeed. The stakes are simply too enormous for humankind in the midst of the turmoil that has now engulfed the world. The spiritual leader of Tibet stands as a beacon for people everywhere. A satisfactory outcome of his struggle will renew humanity's faith in itself in a world rent asunder by so many hatreds and divisions.

The moment the twentieth century mindset is shed, as being totally inadequate, the realisation dawns that the simple issue of the restoration of the Dalai Lama has assumed such extraordinary military dimensions that one is hard put to find any parallel in recent times. The nature of the military build up in Tibet is just not commensurate to the challenge that the Dalai Lama poses. How on earth can a handful of followers of an itinerant monk militarily challenge the might of the Peoples' Republic of China? The very notion is absurd. Whichever way they look at the problem the military dimension should not enter into the reckoning unless the Chinese wish to use Tibet as a launch pad for aggression against India at some future date. That assumption too becomes difficult to comprehend in the case of Tibet. In the eyes of the Government of India, except for not insurmountable differences on the boundary issue, the Tibetan question has been settled once and for all. The Dalai Lama has not advocated an armed uprising and nor would the Indian government countenance such action from Indian soil. Hence, China is very comfortably placed vis-a-vis Tibet at the dawn of the twenty-first century. By not demilitarising Tibet it forces India to militarise the eastern Himalayas. Should over-militarisation again erupt into a major conflagration the 'settled' Tibetan question would automatically stand re-opened, regardless of the outcome of the struggle. The rest of the world acquiesced in the Chinese conquest of Tibet in the 1950s because India did so. Had India challenged the usurpation, the world, without doubt, would have sided with India at that time. China should remain eternally grateful to India for not only serving Tibet to it on a platter, but for compounding the Himalayan blunder by then going on to champion that country's case before the rest of the world, in the difficult years following the communist take-over. Thereafter, India maintained a stoic silence while the genocide in Tibet proceeded apace. Hence, from a geopolitical standpoint it is vital to China's long-term interests to demilitarise Tibet with concomitant demilitarisation of the eastern Himalayas on the part of India. The blueprint for the "demilitarisation of the Himalayas as an ecological imperative" could serve as a basis.[2]

China is already a major force in world affairs. It might one day narrow the gap with the United States in nuclear and missile weaponry. It faces no military threat from India in the coming century; it could, instead, go under from the contradictions and pressures building up internally. Should its leadership, at the dawn of the new millennium, look at the world through a different lens, they would be the first to realise that an historic compromise with the Dalai Lama would automatically relieve pressure on practically all other fronts. The time has come for a great civilisation to turn a supposed adversary into a stout ally, ushering in thereby a new destiny for the region and the world of the 21st century.

## End Notes

1. See also *Liberal Times,* Vol. XI, no. 3, 3/03.
2. For details see Vinod Saighal *Restructuring South Asian Security,* New Delhi, Manas Publications, 2000.

# 3

# Redefining Europe-Asia Security

## Introductory Remarks

The discussion* takes place at a time when neither Europe nor Asia can afford to be mere bystanders to events that could cause cataclysmic upheavals across continents. The superpower casts its giant shadow across the world. At the zenith of its power the USA might set in motion a train of events that could lead to global turmoil on an unmanageable scale. To follow up on aspects of common concern to Europe and Asia in the changing global matrix the discussion is progressed along the following lines: The Backdrop or the Global Matrix; The European Perspective, to include: (i) The Question of Turkish Adhesion to the E.U & (ii) Europe – Russia Relations; An Asian Perspective, to include: (i) Asia: Focus of Global Attention & (ii) Revisiting the Pak-Afghan Cauldron; Some Other Perspectives; Towards a Common Endeavour; Looking Beyond Iraq[1].

## Backdrop

It would be appropriate to take into account the global backdrop against which Europe-Asia security can be

---

* Based on talk delivered on 5 February 2003 at the United Service Institution of India.

redefined for the opening decade of the 21st century. The fast changing global situation does not really permit a longer perspective. Briefly, the dominant strains of the global situation at present can be summarized as:

- East-West rivalry has almost petered out, at least for the time being.
- The military capacities of non-western countries, especially developing countries are too low to mount an effective challenge against US power projection, almost anywhere in the world.
- China could continue to adjust to US projections till the time it has developed a reasonable retaliatory capability.
- Western societies with their higher living standards and built in affluence could show increasing signs of becoming soft in the sense that volunteers for military duty under very harsh climatic or terrain conditions will scarcely be forthcoming. Even conscripts may not show the same enthusiasm as in the past. Therefore, the high-tech military differential becomes an existential imperative for USA and its allies.
- Third World countries unless they become militarily and economically strong will continue to be pushed to the margins of global decision-making.
- A united Europe will increasingly use the political instrument to increase the international competitiveness of its national and transnational enterprises.
- The US has reached the stage where it can propel an arms race or create tension in any part of the globe.
- Capitalist economies are not likely to go to war against each other in the foreseeable future.

- Because of the destructive potential of modern weapon systems the big state actors of the 21st century, namely USA, Western Europe, Russia, China, Japan and India are unlikely to undertake large-scale military operations against each other directly. All these major entities could ultimately develop a joint stake in global stability.
- Non-capitalist societies will continue to constitute the large majority of states around the world. The new global order is not likely to allow for any major improvement in their living conditions. Therefore, hinting that chaos would result in their societies unless the West made major concessions will not obtain any meaningful concessions. For the same reason the gap between the upper income groups and the have-nots will continue to grow; the latter will be pushed to the margins, both within affluent societies as well as in the developing world. It follows therefrom that social integrations are not likely to be brought about by market forces that are in the ascendant today, and will continue to remain in the ascendant for a long time to come.

In the short-term horizon the US does not have strategic concerns beyond Asia that could necessitate large-scale military redeployments. Beyond Asia the concerns generally fall in the non-military category. In Europe these relate to trade relations and the increasing independence in decision-making by the European Union. In Africa they relate to the AIDS burnout and the local conflicts that even during the Cold War did not have extra-regional dimensions, by way of the spread of the fighting. Elsewhere in the Americas the greatest concern remains the possibility of an economic implosion in Latin America.

## The European Perspective

It is worth beginning the analysis of the European perspective with an extract from an article written by two distinguished resident ambassadors representing countries with which India has traditionally enjoyed good relations. The article appeared recently in a leading English daily published from the capital. With a fine rhetorical flourish they concluded by saying: "There is never a dead end in history".*

The debate on the enlargement of the European Union is important for European as well as Asian security. A cohesive European Union with an independent policy, balanced between the unilateralist urges of USA and the security needs of the rest of the world is of equal interest to both sides. Blind adherence to US policies was a compulsion for Western Europe during the Cold War. The Cold War has ended. Europe has moved on. Russia has moved away. The rest of the world has gotten out of the Cold War mindset. America must do the same. It becomes a prerequisite not only for European-Asian security, also for global stability in the new century.

Much has been said and written about the eastward expansion of the European Union. When ten additional members are added, giving it a strength of 25 by 2004, the E.U. will comprise nearly half a billion people—a very large grouping by any standards. Even if it remains at that level it will automatically assume a stature which neither USA nor the rest of the world would be able to ignore, provided that the possibility of externally inspired, unity-shattering fissures is excluded *ab initio*. The discussions on the European Union expansion to date have generally been Euro-centric. The USA has played a role in the debate to

* Dominique Girard and Heimo Richter, 'Akhand Europe', *Times of India*, 22 January 2003.

influence decisions from an American standpoint. There have been few comments about the E.U. enlargement from an Asian standpoint.

In 2004 the expanded European Union—coming into being 13 years after the fall of the Berlin Wall—would stretch from Portugal on the Atlantic coast to the borders of Russia. The ecstatic President of the European Commission, Romano Prodi said that, 'the accession of 10 new member states will bring an end to divisions of Europe'. As things stand the statement would appear to be rather optimistic.

Turkey with a population of nearly 70 million, however, still remains the big question mark. The US has been pushing for the inclusion of Turkey. Why is the USA doing so? In addition to the support that the USA could require from Turkey for its operations in the Middle East or Central Asia, USA's special relationship with it will ensure that with Turkey inside the E.U., the USA retains a strong veto over E.U. policy. It would then have secured both flanks of the E.U. i.e. UK in the west and Turkey at the other end in the southeast. Millions of Turkish citizens now live in Western Europe. The Turkish army is the second largest alliance army after the US. Turkey's understated strategic alliance with Israel helps it gain the support of the powerful pro-Israeli lobbies in the US. To an extent it offsets Syria's hostility to Israel. While pleading the case for entry into the European Union as a full member, Turkish governments have underplayed the linkages that bind them more solidly to Asia. The (second) European phase of Turkey came into the ascendant only after the reforms brought in by Kemal Ataturk. They are skin deep. They represent only 70 years or so of modern Turkish history. They are not deep enough to submerge Turkey's past centrality to Islam in its most glorious period, for the best part of the second millennium after Christ. The Ottoman Empire was the fulcrum of Islamic stability for over 500 years. Possibly, it was with these aspects in mind that the former French President, Valery Giscard d'Estaing, Chairman of the E.U's federal constitution project stated, 'Turkey is not a European country, and that its access to the E.U. would be the end of that organization'. Not surprisingly, his stand won a significant endorsement. He was the recipient of Germany's prestigious Karlspreis (Charlemagne Prize) for 2003. [2]

While the religious angle may continue to predominate there are more important aspects that tend to get ignored. If these are not taken into account they could in the longer term upset the cohesion as well as the equilibrium of an expanded European Union. There are unstated fears that underlie European concerns while considering the Turkish request. It is a moot point whether the persistence with which the US has been pushing Turkey's case for entry into the European Union works to Turkey's advantage or otherwise. Already the European Union is hamstrung to an extent by the British ambivalence between its ties to the US and its links to the European Union. Europe would be unable to get along harmoniously with a similar dilemma at the other end of an expanded European Union. The demography of Turkey's adherence might also prove worrying to the European Union. Recently, Spain indicated its desire to accept up to a million immigrants from Latin American nations with historic ties to Spain. The new settlers coming into Spain would be free to cross over into any of the West European countries. Should Turkey become a full member of the European Union, similar facilities will have to be afforded to that country. Once inside Europe as an equal partner Turkey would not take kindly to any discrimination.

Turkey itself should examine its approach *de novo*. With its past heritage of greatness it is primarily an Asian power. It need not hanker after a grouping that looks askance at the prospect. Were the issue to be re-examined dispassionately by the Turks they might find that they could become the prime movers for the revitalisation of the Middle East in the new century, should they choose to look Eastward rather than Westward.

Increasingly, in the years ahead, Europe will be compelled to come to terms with the emerging global reality. The might of the US power, notwithstanding, the Old Continent will have to decide as to where it is headed. Because, hereafter, with each passing year the resemblance—and remembrance—would fade of the decades of the Cold War period when Europe felt that it had no choice other than being tied to US apron strings as part of a coalition that faced grave challenges from Soviet military might as well as from the global advance of the communist ideology. Both threats have ceased to exist. In their absence, should Europe continue to follow the old pattern of subservience to US interests, not only would it diminish Europe, it would also undermine Europe–Asian security, as well as global stability. Therefore, the new course charted by the European Union has overriding importance for Asia. Europe has no enemies at the beginning of the 21st century, whereas America's enemies are legion. They are multiplying with each passing day. Where does this leave Europe? Is it going to be a voice of moderation or will it continue as a blind supporter of policies that clearly threaten the world? Across the face of Europe, European men and women perceive the dangers posed to humanity through the exercise of unbridled unilateralism. The question that needs to be asked is 'are European leaders responding to the sentiment of their populations'. After centuries of strife the people of Europe do not want war. War may not take place in Europe. It could come to Europe in many other ways. Europe abuts the continents of Asia and Africa. The USA is oceans away, literally so, across the

Atlantic and the Pacific. These oceans allow it to sally forth and interfere decisively in the affairs of the non-American continents of the world. They also allow it to pull back into an isolation mode while the destructive forces unleashed ravage the continents of Asia-Europe and Africa.

Will Europe develop into a super state? To answer this question there is a need to examine whether Europe has a capacity to act autonomously – in foreign policy, in its economic policy as well as with a military capability to match. An increasing number of Europeans are worried about the fast deteriorating military situation concerning Iraq. In European forums a consensus seems to be emerging that the E.U. should speak with one voice and that member states should coordinate their strategy on issues relating to Iraq, energy (oil) and global trade. Germany has already let it be known that its troops would not participate in Iraq.

## Europe–Russia Relations

Russian leaders have watched with misgiving NATO's continued thrust up to and around Russia. They feel helpless in the face of this eastward expansionist urge. Like the Chinese they too prefer to remain silent. For the time being that is. As NATO expands deeper to embrace the former Soviet Warsaw Pact members it may find that it has taken on more than it can chew. The expansion may create problems in the years ahead that NATO had neither anticipated nor bargained for. At the end of it all the snowballing process may break the very cohesion of NATO, which was as much a basis of its strength as its military might against a foe that could be assigned a shape, size and name. Now, the foes have become amorphous. Europe had several options open to it in the post-Cold War phase when it decided to expand its security space at the cost of a Russia reeling from the break up of the Soviet Union.

Notwithstanding the spirit of co-operation that has been shown by one side and accepted as a right by the other, being the victors of the Cold War, there are dark clouds on their common horizon in Europe and Asia that could undermine the relationship. Briefly, these include, *inter alia*:

- The US has yet to repeal the Jackson-Vannik Amendment, which is a Cold War law that denies fair access for Russian goods to the American market as long as the Kremlin continues to deny Soviet Jews the right to emigrate – an issue that can hardly be termed as relevant today.
- Economic depression on a global scale whose consequences may be difficult to foresee at this juncture.
- A war in the Middle East that either spins out of control or ends up by putting Russia at a greater disadvantage, than it is presently.
- The US not honouring Iraq's oil concessions and debts to Russia in the post-intervention setting.
- Competition over oil resources and pipeline routes in Central Asia and the Caucasus that further sideline Russia.

For Western Europe – as distinct from NATO – the co-optation of Russia into an integrated European security environment must remain one of the foremost challenges for creating a more stable global order. For Asia and Europe the future of Russia could well become the cornerstone of geopolitical stability as well as economic prosperity for the Eurasian landmass. Its geographic as well as historic contiguity mandates an environment of 'integrated co-operation' for the well-being of both these continents.

## An Asian Perspective

### Asia–Focus of Global Action

Asia has become the center of global focus for several reasons. These include:

- Asia now has, or will soon have, the single largest concentration of economic power. In the not too distant future it could outstrip the economic power of the other economic power blocs, namely, USA and Europe.
- The bulk of the demographic mass of the world is concentrated in Asia. This demographic mass could one day represent a much larger middle class numbering a billion plus people whose combined consumption potential would ensure the viability of a vast range of global industries and businesses. In addition, the same demographic mass represents a large pool of cheap labour that fuels the economic growth of many multinationals based in USA and Europe.
- Asia contains the largest known reserves of hydrocarbon energy.
- The countries or entities that could rival US power are mostly located in Asia.

Hence, it will be seen that the demographic – economic interface of the 21st century, as perceived at this point in time, will continue to militate in favour of Asia being the center point of geo-economic interest of the world for the best part of the century. It is axiomatic that this locus of the largest economic potential of the world will continue to attract the interest of the non-Asian world in both economic and military terms. During the early period of the Cold War the two superpowers and to an extent China could be deemed to have been the cause of geopolitical instability in the region. After the Cold War the US military presence in the region, especially in East and Southeast Asia, had resulted in regional stability to the extent that it became a dampener on China's expansionist potential. Post-September 11, 2001 the US military build up in Afghanistan, Central Asia and elsewhere has dramatically altered the geo-strategic balance in Asia.

The essential items of Asian security for the coming decades will require:

- Reunification of North and South Korea based on the phased demilitarisation of North Korea and its co-optation into the enlarged South Korea economic zone; somewhat similar to the exercise that was undertaken by West Germany to co-opt the economically backward East German state after the fall of the Berlin Wall.
- South Asian stability based on co-optation of the smaller South Asian economies into the larger Indian economy.
- Demilitarisation of the Himalayas, autonomy for Tibet, and settlement of the China-India boundary dispute.
- Confederation of Central Asian Republics – on the lines of the E.U. - guaranteed by Russia, China, India, E.U. and USA.
- Stability in Afghanistan.
- De-jehadisation of Pakistan; failing which neutralization of Pakistan.
- Prevention of the spread of militant/orthodox Islam in Southeast, South and Central Asia.
- Re-integrating Iran into the global mainstream.

It will be seen from the tabulation given above that if a line were to be drawn across Eurasia from North to

South along the 76º meridian the regions East of that line could develop a formidable geo-economic stability and even harmony should the four major powers of the region i.e. Russia, China, Japan and India decide to move in that direction. A joint initiative of this nature will not only enhance the prosperity of these major powers individually, but usher in geo-strategic and geo-economic harmony that could easily guarantee a steady growth for the region till well into the century and beyond. Since there need not be any insurmountable tensions between these four major powers—bilaterally or as a collectivity—there is no reason for them not to come together to form a solid Central, South, Southeast and East Asian stability base. Once the process is started, it could automatically become the basis for global stability. The collective force – demographic, geographic, economic and political—of these four countries is greater than the collective force of any other region or grouping in the world. It is a force that represents innate stability, as it does not desire extra-regional expansion. Hence, a summit conference between Russia, China, Japan and India should be held at the earliest to define the parameters of the new Eastern Asia stability. Countries to the West of the 76° meridian have been deliberately kept aside for the present as the West Asian region is still far from reaching the same base level of *inter se* security and stability as obtains in the eastern half of Asia, barring the issues of Taiwan and North Korea. These might become less intractable if addressed jointly by the 'Asia 4' (China, India, Russia & Japan), thereby excluding non-Asian interference.

The Palestine-Israel standoff has been artificially projected as the sole cause of West Asian unrest, thereby conveniently submerging the other causes and preventing them from being examined with the same degree of transparency as obtains for the Palestinian question. First of all, the Palestine question directly concerns Egypt, Israel,

Lebanon, Syria, Jordan and the Palestinians themselves. Other Muslim countries are not concerned directly, or even indirectly. Emotions have been whipped up over the years to hide the deficiencies of their own intractable problems and the systemic failures of their systems of governance, especially after the oil price increase of the early 1970s. While there is no question that an equitable solution to the Palestine question is the prime need of the hour, the Palestinian issue need not arouse the ire of the entire Muslim world simply because victims happen to be from the same faith. Should that be the case, there should have been an outrage of several orders of magnitude higher than the outrage against Israel when the Pakistan army in less then one year slaughtered nearly three million East Bengalis (Bangladeshis) who were fellow Muslims from the same country. In fact, if measured against the time and scale factors, these killings in just 10-12 months rank higher than the pogroms carried out by Stalin in Russia and Hitler's killings of the Jews in Europe from 1939-1945.

Therefore, while accepting that the Palestine question will remain a flashpoint, the other factors leading to continued instability in the Middle East need also to be kept in mind. Briefly, these could be summarized as follows:

- The non-democratic set-up of almost all the regimes in the region.
- Over-emphasis on religious orthodoxy that keeps the population of the region outside the global mainstream of the Twenty-first century.
- The inequitable distribution of the wealth that came into the region from soaring oil prices.
- Over-militarisation of the region.
- The Shia-Sunni schism.
- The geopolitical ambitions of some countries in the region.

- Lack of investment in health and education.
- Continued suppression of women.
- The horrendous population growth in regions of low productivity.

## Revisiting Afghanistan–Pakistan

In undertaking an analysis of European-Asian security a reference has inevitably to be made to the Pakistan-Afghanistan region. Because unless stability returns to Afghanistan and unless Pakistan's own role as the epicenter of terrorism diminishes significantly these two countries will continue to cast a disproportionate shadow on world affairs. A few additional points that need to be made can be summarized as follows:

- The chances of stability returning to Afghanistan would go up if interference from Pakistan were to be excluded. There are many ways of limiting such interference.
- It may become necessary for the world to put a *cordon sanitaire* around Pakistan should it continue to export terror and remain the hub for the export of nuclear know-how. Here it must be mentioned that while the world was dismayed by the coming to light of transfer of nuclear know-how from Pakistan to North Korea it is surprising that to date the inference has not been made that Pakistan would have been obliged to have first transferred the know-how to Saudi Arabia and Libya who were the principle backers of the so-called 'Islamic' bomb programme at its inception in the 1970s. A significant amount of funding to initiate the programme was made available by these countries. In fact, they became the principle equity stakeholders in this dubious venture.

In the past India had been excluded from the six plus two conclaves on Afghanistan on the ground that it did not have contiguity with Afghanistan. Surprisingly, India went along with this line of thinking. Because it had not roundly denounced Soviet intervention it felt diffident. Hereafter, India must forcefully project its direct interest in Afghanistan at par with any of the countries bordering Afghanistan. For historical, cultural and many other reasons India and Afghanistan have had a major influence on each other for several millennia going back to the period of the Kushan Empire, and even earlier. Great dynasties that ruled over India in the second millennium came from Afghanistan and Central Asia. In the post-colonial world Afghanistan's golden period of peace and tranquility—as most Afghans readily concede—was during Zahir Shah's reign when Indian influence was at its height. There was no interference by India, only help for modernization and nation building. Thereafter, India was denied direct access to Afghanistan. However, a mere 50 years of partitioning of the subcontinent do not diminish the bonds that stretch over thousands of years. It is tantamount to saying that the Soviet occupation of Eastern Europe diminished the historical bonds between them and the rest of Europe. Western Europe has reasserted its right. So will India. Henceforth, India maintains that it has the greatest direct interest in the stability of Afghanistan. It shall take all measures to ensure that its historic right remains untrammeled. When the issue is closely examined it will be seen that it is in the interest of USA, Russia, Central Asia, Iran and the Western world to accord this primacy to India. At the very least it is not going to allow failing states exporting terror to attempt to abridge this right.

Pakistan rejected India's nuclear no-first-use agreement. Pakistan supports the proposal for a nuclear weapons free zone in South Asia. The point to note here as far as the global community is concerned is that Pakistan is not an independent player in these formulations. Pakistan has closely co-ordinated its nuclear and missile policies with those of China and North Korea. Pakistan, in fact, did not need to carry out the 1998 tests after India's Pokharan II tests. It is generally well known in Western circles that China had made available nuclear weapons know-how to Pakistan as early as the 1980's. Pakistan could already have transferred nuclear materials to Saudi Arabia, Libya and non-state actors. Pakistan remains a surrogate for China on the sub-continent. Its projections, often on behalf of China, are amazingly naïve. Without a nuclear and missile shield India's asymmetry in relation to China would increase to an unmanageable degree. Pakistan, even without its nuclear shield would be comfortable with the conventional inferiority with non-nuclear India knowing that China could resume the flow of nuclear and missile weaponry to Pakistan at will, as it has been doing in the past. India would be left high and dry. Additionally, India could be pushed around by China. These aspects are highlighted so that in the changing circumstances the European Union, which, taking its cue from the USA, has been backing several initiatives of this type in the past should stand disabused. Artificially weakening India through the artfully contrived Pakistan – China projections would be a geo-strategic negativity for Europe while redefining European–Asian security in the face of the growing military and economic strength of China. The rise of Islamic fundamentalism threatens Europe far more than USA, owing to its geographic contiguity to the Muslim world and its larger Muslim population.

Amazingly there is still talk that the US requires Pakistan's support to continue its operations in Afghanistan. In future it is the reverse proposition that could be truer. The Taliban and Al-Qaeda cadres along with their leaders that the US was looking for in Afghanistan have all ex-filtrated to their secure home base of Pakistan–whence they came. Hunting them is going to be far more problematic than was the case when they were located in Afghanistan. The Afghans have had enough of the Taliban dispensation. Not so in Pakistan, where they are securely ensconced in the lap of their local jehadi sympathisers who nurtured them. Hence, now it is Afghanistan that becomes the US base for launching operations into Pakistan, both for hunting the Taliban/Al-Qaeda escapees as also to launch subsequent operations into that country, should the situation deteriorate further.

## Some Other Perspectives

It would be worth recalling two interesting US formulations –both very recent:

'Even if Saddam commits suicide in front of television cameras, US will still invade Iraq in January 2003.' – Professor Immanuel Wallerstein, a well-known left liberal intellectual in USA.[3]

"It is a simple reality that the US power is unrivaled and will remain so for the foreseeable future. Yet, this power does not give the United States control over global affairs". -Richard N. Haass.[4]

European nations had started re-assessing their position vis-à-vis USA with respect to the rest of the world. 9/11 reunited them. It turned out to be a temporary interlude. Going beyond 9/11 Europe cannot tread the American path. Whether they are able to put it in so many words or not the question uppermost in the minds of the West European countries today is not whether they see a parting of ways with USA, but when that break occurs. The break in this case does not signify mistrust or hostility. The Western countries remain solidly allied to USA, but not in the military sense of the term or in the policies that they are likely to pursue to safeguard European interests and European security. Europe no longer faces a military threat, as was the case in the Cold War years. Other threats have emerged. They may or may not require a military response. They may or may not require a joint Europe–USA high-tech devastation of other parts of the globe.

After 9/11 Russia whole-heartedly supported the American intervention in Afghanistan and even facilitated the advent of US forces in Central Asia. Russia muted its response to the unilateral US withdrawal from the 1972 ABM Treaty. However, with increasing American intransigence over Iraq and US insensitivity to the views of the other members of the UN Security Council, Russia may decide to modify its course. It is unlikely that Russia will abandon its pro-US approach altogether unless pushed to the extreme. Nonetheless, new thrusts toward Asia, especially with China and India seem to be in the offing. China and India between them buy over 70 percent of all Russian military production and 75 percent of all Russian arms exports. That is not all. Russia's trade with China jumped from a little over $ 10 billion in 2001 to a projected $ 12 billion in 2003. Trade with India is also likely to increase. Therefore, India and China remain crucial to Russia's re-emergence as a national power.

While Japan and the US have been co-operating in dealing with North Korea it has to be realised that looking ahead Japan will seek to strike a balance between its close alliance of the last 50 years with its US ally and the need for reestablishing its Asian relationship as an independent player, de-linked from the compulsions of the USA, the G-8 or the Western alliance. When Japan undertakes this exercise it will find that it could become an important determinant for reshaping the destiny of Asia. Evidently, Japan while wishing to distance itself from US policies might not wish to sever the bonds of an alliance that was instrumental in projecting it to the stature of an economic giant while sheltering under the US security umbrella. What would worry Japan and should cause anxiety to thinking Japanese is the fact that continuing in the same mould diminishes its voice in international circles.

Seeing the benefits that have accrued to both China and Japan from large Japanese investments on the mainland, Japan could enter into a new relationship with India which could be the next domain for investments by Japan, both as countervailing economic strategy as also the harbinger of new geo-strategic equations that guarantee stability in the eastern half of the Asian continent in an arc going from New Delhi – Singapore – Jakarta – Hanoi – Tokyo – Beijing – Seoul – Pyongyang – up to Vladivostok. None of the likely outcomes need to be viewed with disfavour by USA. In the long-term they would become the cornerstone of a new global stability order, which could be underpinned by Russia and the European Union to the north and by USA as part of its global outreach.

## Towards A Common Endeavour

### Europe–Asia Jointmanship

"A religious society perceives evil in terms of moral choice, but the free will of a secular society seeks the causes of evil in political and psychological terms". – Javier Solana.

Typically, human security comprises two major elements i.e. freedom from fear and freedom from want. Taking these elements as the basis of this discussion it will readily be seen that whereas in Europe freedom from want has diminished greatly in the decades following World War II, in Asia it remains the single most important concern for a large percentage of the population. Fear thereby gets subsumed in the basic concern for survival. More recently, especially with the rise of global terrorism in the form of

Islamic jehad, many countries in Europe that felt safe under the military might of NATO and its nuclear umbrella now sense a rising surge of fear. More so, since it now requires less and less effort to kill a larger number of people, or to shatter the tranquility of people who felt safely ensconced in their post-Cold War security.

Beside USA the entities that are likely to play a major role in the shaping of world affairs in the $21^{st}$ century are all situated in the Europe-Asia region. These are the European Union, Russia, China, Japan and India. Regardless of all else, their coming together to take a common approach on some of the most pressing global concerns of today could go a long way in righting the distortions that have crept into world affairs. The effects of these distortions would be felt most keenly in the Eurasian landmass. The main areas where a commonality of approach can be worked out would, *inter alia* be:

- Strengthening of the United Nations.
- Reform of the UN Security Council.
- Prevention of the militarisation of space.
- Moving back towards phased universal nuclear disarmament.
- Strengthening the protocols for chemical and biological weapons conventions.
- Strengthening of the International Criminal Court.
- Redeployment of funds for health and education in developing countries.
- Joint approach to tackle global terrorism.
- Joint approach for persuading the US to abjure unilateralism and to abide by the global conventions painstakingly arrived at by the comity of nations in the $20^{th}$ century.

- Preventing further ecological destruction of the planet.
- Stabilisation of the human population on the planet.

The big powers of the Europe-Asia region that have the ability to reshape the world order should they co-ordinate their approach on the major global issues can bring durable peace to their respective continents as well as the adjoining continent of Africa. Their joint approach does not *ipso facto* become anti-Americanism, so to say. It would merely mean that these entities have come to the conclusion that unless they take a stand on some of the major issues in the larger interest of humankind the planetary stresses being generated by the global policies in the ascendant—largely at the behest of the remaining superpower—could lead to an irreversible global decline by the turn of the century, or even before.

The European Union could play a pivotal role provided it displays a unity of purpose. There are several reasons for assigning a greater value to the role of the European Union at this juncture than that assigned to Russia, China, Japan or India because of the fact that regardless of the construction that US may put on it, its hegemonistic tendencies that could de-stabilize the existing world order are predicated on the continuing support of Western Europe and Japan, as was the case throughout the second half of the 20th century. Should either of these two i.e. the European Union or Japan decide to dissociate themselves from US policies that run counter to the spirit of the age, it would not be possible for the latter to continue in the same vein for any length of time. Even its Star Wars and anti-missile shields are based on intermediate relay/radar locations or ground support from some European countries, Japan, Australia and Canada. Of late, the USA has let it be known that should it not get the support of Western Europe it could still move ahead unilaterally. These statements taken at face value presuppose the following:

- That UK will continue to remain firm in the Anglo-American concord.
- That the USA would be able to continue to influence individual European countries to follow separate policies. For example, presently Italy, Spain and Poland have been co-opted into the American system for US geopolitical projections or unilateral actions.
- That even if West European unity or European Union unity did take place, Canada and Japan would continue to support US actions.
- That Turkey would remain available as a base for launching forces in Central Asia or the Middle East.
- That the Pakistan military could be dragooned to support US actions under a military dictator wholly dependent upon the USA for his continuing in power, or even his survival.

There are many lesser aspects that could be enumerated in this respect. Suffice to say, that their occasional differences notwithstanding, as in the case of strong German opposition to US unilateralism in Iraq, the USA is convinced of its ability to keep its Western allies and Japan in tow if the stakes were to be sufficiently raised. Or, to put it differently, if the USA could raise the ante to such an extent that its European allies would have no choice but to remain on the side of USA in its unilateralist interventions. It is for this reason that the question of the enlargement of the European Union needs to be looked at more closely by the public of the European countries as well from the capitals of Russia, China, Japan and India.

## Looking Beyond Iraq

The attention of the world is focused on Iraq and the irreversible momentum being built up by relentless US deployment in West Asia. There appears to be a consensus that regardless of all else America will get its way, the difference being only in detail. The USA's desire to obtain control over the Iraqi oil resources has been discussed threadbare. In the long-term interest of Europe–Asian security the more important issues, looking beyond Iraq that need to be considered include:

- Is Iraq the end of the US cycle of intervention that began with the Gulf War over a decade ago or is it the beginning of a new cycle?
- If the latter, what else is the US likely to do post-Iraq?
- What effect will the US action have on Europe and Asia?
- Is there a hidden agenda, which the world is not yet aware of?
- What are the larger global ramifications of the US actions?

With its intervention in Iraq the US has also painted itself into a corner. It cannot simply pull back and go away. The Bush administration, possibly deliberately, has railroaded the US and most of its allies into a tunnel from which exit is possible only through the other end of the tunnel. If the USA does not succeed in pacifying Iraq it would be seriously undermining its military credibility. Hence, it is unlikely that the USA will turn back without achieving its aims.

## Ecological Ramifications

Of the many concerns raised about a US invasion of Iraq, the overriding concern, which has not received the attention it deserves relates to the ecological destruction that could be taking place in the region. Inexplicably, none of the countries most concerned i.e. Iran, Turkey, Syria, Jordan, Saudi Arabia and the Gulf states have explained to their people that the high intensity war launched by USA—even though below the nuclear threshold—could have a devastating effect on their region, including the marine ecology of the entire Persian Gulf. The deep earth penetrators and other deadly munitions that the US has used and the quantities in which these have been used, not only destroy the assets targeted, they leave residues that would affect the populations of these countries as well as the flora and fauna of the region for generations to come. It is highly likely that the effects would be felt as far afield as the Mediterranean region and Central Asia.

Reports have recently been coming in about what is being referred to as ABC, or the Asian Brown Cloud. Earlier it had been referred to as the Indian Ocean haze. While the issue may have been put on the back burner at the United Nations Environment Programme (UNEP) Conference held in Nairobi in February 2003, the so-called haze or the brown cover has been attributed to several contributory factors that include the use of inefficient wood burning stoves, deforestation and the like. Not many people at the time mentioned that the haze, if it exists, could be attributed to the intense US bombardment in Afghanistan and later on in Iraq. In these circumstances there could hardly be any doubt that under the conditions prevailing in the desert the dust haze comprising fine sand and explosives' residue could hang over the region for a long time. It would lead to bronchial and respiratory diseases in a large segment of the population in Iraq and the neighbouring countries.

Ordinary people around the world coming out to protest against the war in Iraq do not have a partisan outlook in this regard. The people demonstrating – at least in the non-Muslim countries i.e. in Europe and America—cannot be labeled as anti-American. Their concerns relating to the planetary stresses that are being generated go deeper than the geopolitical manoeuverings of the governing elites of their countries. It clearly brings out that the establishments running these countries are out of sync with their own people, who are coming out in increasingly larger numbers to protest against the intervention in Iraq. Other ways would have to be found to deal with the menace of proliferation of weapons of mass destruction. The country representatives of the nations at the UN and the Secretary General could give thought to convening a special session to go into the ecological ramifications of the invasion of Iraq.

## Concluding Remarks

Across the world, from the east to the west and from countries in the north to those in the south people are turning out in large numbers to protest against American unilateral actions in Iraq without a mandate from the UN. They are spontaneous protests by people concerned about the well-being of humanity. Hardly any of the protesters can be said to be supporters of the Iraqi strongman. More protests are taking place in countries that are closely allied to USA. Americans themselves demonstrated in many cities. There has not been a single march anywhere in the world supporting the designs of the US establishment. The comments from around the world relate to US designs on Iraq's oil wealth and for American power projection in the Middle East and Central Asia. Surprisingly, the most important issue that concerns the world has generally receded into the background. The US action, taking place unilaterally, could turn out to be the most significant global event after World War II. It would, in a manner of speaking, signify the demise of the post-war order that gave birth to the United Nations and the Bretton Woods institutions.

The losers would be the victors of World War II who shaped the world body and subordinated it to their interests for over half a century. The implications would be the most grave for USA itself. After the US action the sanctity of the veto power of the five permanent members would cease to have any relevance for the global order. A new and uncertain phase has commenced for the unfolding world history.

In that respect we would not be witnessing the 'end of history'. It could mark the beginning of the decline of the greatest power that the world has known, leaving in its wake a vacuum far more threatening to the global order than the superpower hegemony that preceded it. The discussion started with a paradox. It ends with another paradox: presently the world is as dependent on the US for a balanced global order as the US is on the other nations to maintain that order.

## Postscript

As the European leaders made plans for their annual Christmas and New Year vacation the Italian Prime Minister Silvio Berlusconi threw in the towel after failing to get a consensus on compromise proposals designed to unblock the deadlock over voting rights. Talks on the first European Union constitution that broke down in mid-December 2003 are unlikely to resume in earnest until the year 2005, when the six-month rotating presidency of the European Union is taken over by Luxembourg in the first half of 2005. Ireland, which took over the six-month rotating presidency of the EU bloc in January 2004 would also be holding consultations to suggest a way forward. The European Union was plunged into crisis after a two-year-old divide to forge a new constitution collapsed, leaving the bloc without the badly needed reforms to equip it for its biggest expansion yet. Intensive attempts by the EU's Italian presidency to broker a deal foundered on fierce demands by Poland and Spain to retain the generous voting rights they secured in the Nice Treaty three years ago. The collapse of what should have been an historic summit shook the wealthy 15 nation EU bloc, barely five months before it was due to admit ten new members – mainly former communist countries –in the biggest enlargement in its five decade history. Not unsurprisingly, the French President Jacques Chirac called for "pioneer group" of core countries to forge ahead with closer integration in defence, economic policy and justice. He, of course, denied that it would lead to the European Union nations being segregated into first– and second–class Europeans. He maintained that the core countries forging ahead would allow Europe to move faster, thus setting an example for the rest to follow. The close ally of France, the German Chancellor Gerhard Schroeder took a similar line.

It could be more than a coincidence that the voting right battles pitted two strong supporters of the US-led invasion of Iraq, Spain and Poland against the two most outspoken opponents of the war in Europe, namely Germany and France. As to what role the US may have played behind the scenes in stiffening the resolve of Spain and Poland remains a matter for conjecture. What lies beyond conjecture, however, is the determination of France and Germany with Belgium and Luxembourg in tow to carry the battle for supremacy in the European Union through to its logical conclusion. It could hardly be lost upon the leaders of France and Germany that at the grass roots, practically the whole of Europe from the Atlantic to the Urals is united against the unilateralist tendency of USA. Even in the UK, while Tony Blair remains steadfast with the US ally, President George W. Bush, public opinion in the UK is definitely turning away from the policies adopted by the British government. It is a trend that could become irreversible.

## End Notes

1. Published in the Journal of *United Service Institution of India*, vol. CXXXIII, no. 551, January-March 2003.
2. *The Statesman*, World Briefs, 16 December 2002.
3. *The Daily Star*-Reproduced in *The Statesman*, 22 January 2003.
4. Director, Policy Planning Staff, US Department of State at the CII Partnership Summit in Hyderabad on 7 January 2003.
5. Thomas L. Friedman writing in the *New York Times* mentions that roughly 75 per cent of Poles oppose the deployment of Polish troops in Iraq. (Reproduced in the *Indian Express*, 29 December 2003).

# 4

## *Preventing a Repeat of Iraq in Iran

Any discussion on Iran has to take off from the situation in the Middle East as it is now. Whichever way the main antagonists i.e. America and the forces that they are fighting see it, to the rest of the world it causes concern. The chances of it spinning out of control are fairly strong, even if the USA were to hand the situation over unconditionally to the UN or to the Iraqis. In order to find a satisfactory way out of the impasse there would appear to be three main pathways for doing so. The first would be to follow the shopworn geopolitical pathway in which nations follow their own interest regardless of the consequences for the rest of the world. Non-state actors linked to global terrorism have also started emulating this course of action. The second pathway would be for the UN Security Council, acting independently, to get a grip on the situation. The third pathway could be for the collectivity of nations in the region to determine a course that leads to a form of resolution that might bring about a degree of stability to the region as a whole.

* Talk delivered at the United Service Institution of India, New Delhi on 10 December 2003.

In the years since the events of 9/11 two major groupings appear to have suffered considerable setback to their grand designs. The first was the Pakistan–Saudi Arabia axis that was pushing for an extreme form of regressive Islam in regions beyond their shores. Many people blame US policies for the rise of Islamic fundamentalism. It can quite as easily be argued that the pushing of Islamic orthodoxy by its prime movers, Pakistan and Saudi Arabia since about the 1970s, well before the 'clash of civilizations' theory gained currency, could also have been a contributory factor. Regressive Islamic theology taken to the extreme spawned the likes of Al-Qaeda, Taliban and like-minded jehadi elements. The latter now seem to have pushed the first movers into the background. These designs met with concerted global action after the Twin Tower bombings and the passing of UNSC Resolution 1373. The other major grouping, the Anglo-American alliance, intervened decisively in Afghanistan to deliver a crushing blow to the Taliban regime with minimal casualties to the coalition forces. Thereafter, seeing that success came easy with the use of high-tech weapons for which their adversaries had no matching weaponry, the Anglo-Americans went on to invade Iraq with equal ease. The post-Iraq victory phase has turned out to be a setback to their designs. Notwithstanding the setbacks, neither grouping is likely to give up its long-term goals. The respective reverses might force them to stop the expansion and even perhaps to recoil temporarily. Both entities are likely to reassess their strategy, bring in the necessary changes, and re-launch their offensives at a time of their choosing, even if it entailed a delay of several years. It would be imprudent for the world not to be alive to the possibility of the threat again reemerging from these sources, possibly in a more menacing form.

There are quite a few lesser conflicts around the world. Most of them are not world threatening. On a truly global scale there are only two sets of forces that have developed the capacity and the will – even obduracy, one might say - to actually go for each other's jugular across the world, namely Islamic jehad and its nemesis USA. The reverse proposition could be equally true, i.e., Islamic jehad is becoming the great spoiler of the US expansionist urge in the Middle East and Central Asia. As things stood at the end of 2003, neither side had the capacity to completely checkmate or destroy the other.

Worried by the mayhem resulting from the fundamental conflict of these two irreconcilably antagonistic forces, concerned international groupings are emerging to try and check, in the first instance, the unilateral interventionist urges of the remaining superpower. Outside the UN, which is unable to assert itself the credible new alignments discernible on the horizon are:

- China, Russia, India conclave;
- The Old Europe or the France-Germany-Belgium conclave;
- Germany-France-Russia conclave.

There may be other axes in the offing. Leaving aside the newer economic groupings that are emerging those mentioned above can be seen to be the principal ones. All of them can be said to have a commonality of purpose, which can succinctly be stated as:

- None of them are anti-USA per se;
- All of them wish to preserve their bilateral relations with USA;
- The main reason for their coming together is to attempt to curb the expansionist zeal of USA and to restore global harmony;

- All of them would like to see the UN having a greater role in global security.
- None of these groupings, individually or collectively, would be in a position to fill the vacuum should there be a catastrophic decline in US power in the world. Hence, at this juncture, the emphasis remains on tempering rather than demolishing US power.

Proceeding from these introductory remarks the discussion progresses with the analysis under the following heads:

- A **recapitulation** of the situation in Iraq at the end of 2003;
- Recapitulation of the situation in the regional context;
- The US situation at the beginning of 2004;
- What could happen should the US decide to intervene unilaterally in Iran;
- Co-opting Iran for stability in the Middle East;
- Looking beyond Afghanistan-Iraq and the other countries in the region.

## A Recap of the Iraq situation

The casualties suffered by the US troops on the ground in Iraq are generally being numbered in physical terms i.e. the number of US soldiers killed in Iraq since victory was declared. In actual fact, the psychological devastation of the young American soldiers serving in Iraq is the greater casualty whose negative effects will be felt by American civil society for a long time to come.*

* The writer had spoken on this aspect at a BBC interview at Bush House in London on 16 September 2003.

In military terms the US started losing the battle, in a manner of speaking, when they allowed, post-Iraq intervention, the Islamic fundamentalists and others opposing them to fight the Americans on the ground of their own choosing i.e. in Iraq itself; where the Americans present over a hundred thousand targets to them almost daily. Doubtless, they can reduce the figure exposed to their enemies by a few thousand by digging themselves deeper into the ground or surrounding themselves with more layers of fencing. In the process they lose their freedom of manoeuvre by hunkering down into a ghetto-like mentality, both physical and mental. At the same time while the US troops, who remain the prime target for their enemies, generally limit themselves to their fortresses or sally out in their phalanx-like task forces based around tanks, planes, helicopter gunships and Humvees, those who oppose them have a free run throughout Iraq. Every US soldier killed raises the morale of the Islamic fundamentalists everywhere in the world. Iraq is the tonic, which has allowed them to overcome the demoralization of their earlier defeats in Afghanistan, Iraq and elsewhere. As things stand their morale and mobility will increase in direct proportion to the decrease in US morale and mobility. Although initially the opposition to the US presence might have centered around Saddam Hussein, it is more than likely that other anti-US groupings, better organized, within and outside Iraq might soon eclipse Saddam Hussein-centered opposition on which the US has been concentrating, thereby virtually giving a free hand to those globally organized to hit US interests.*

Taken together, the US policies in Iraq and the situation in Iraq pose the greatest threat to Saudi Arabia. The Saudi government forces may be able to target fundamentalist

* This becomes especially so after the capture of Saddam Hussein.

groups opposed to them within Saudi Arabia. The latter have now adequate sanctuaries in Iraq, where they can fall back, refurbish and again sally out, practically at will.

The Bush administration launched its war against Iraq because, additionally, it intended to make the country the new base for long-term military operations in the Gulf region. After the attacks on the US in September 2001, it realized it would have to withdraw troops from Saudi Arabia. It was then that it decided on Iraq as its new long-term base of operations. It could be an important reason why America is so opposed to a complete transfer of sovereignty to the Iraqis or the UN. A sovereign Iraq might tell the US to withdraw from the country. As long as America remains an occupying force in Iraq, political stability there is unlikely. Without political stability, Iraq's economic recovery is unlikely as well.

According to Jeffrey D Sachs, the biggest costs in Iraq are not for reconstruction but for US troops. America is paying an astounding $51 billion per year to station 140,000 troops in the country, a staggering cost of around $360,000 per soldier per year. The US could save itself tens of billions of dollars per year by withdrawing its troops from Iraq. If the US were then to give just a fraction of the financial saving to Iraq in 2004, there would be plenty of incremental revenues to run the Iraqi government and to support the recovery of oil production. [1]

Without going into the nature, necessity, or intensity of the US incursion into the region it can almost be stated as a truism that what happens next would to a large extent be contingent on what the USA does next. Taking Iraq first, the ground situation being what it is, the US can be said to have the following broad options:

- Continue along the present lines with mid-term corrections, based on its assessment of the situation;
- Place the country under UN Security Council control substantively and unambiguously;

- Attempt to get on top of the situation by bigger military deployment and/or more lethal high tech retaliation, which apparently it has started. *
- Pull out after suffering unacceptable casualties, leaving the country and the region in bigger chaos;
- Any variation of the above.

Not getting into a detailed discussion of the options just spelled out, it would be reasonable to assume that at this point in time the prospects of the USA being able to stabilize the situation to its satisfaction in desirable time frames seem bleak. In the first flush of a walkover victory after moving into Baghdad, US policy-makers immediately set about warning Syria and Iran that they could be next. It set alarm bells ringing around the world - both amongst the traditional allies of USA and those opposed to US policies. Ipso facto the nations most threatened by the likelihood of further US action have thereafter developed a vested interest in Iraqi instability. Within the region, the countries that had reason to fear US designs were Syria,

* For example, Patrick Cockburn, writing in the *London Independent* of October 12 revealed that "U.S. soldiers, driving bulldozers with jazz blaring from the loudspeakers, have uprooted ancient groves of date palms as well as orange and lemon trees in central Iraq as part of a new policy of collective punishment of farmers who do not give information about guerillas attacking U.S. troops." Earlier in November, a Black Hawk helicopter was shot down killing all six U.S. soldiers abroad. In retaliation, U.S. troops backed by Bradley fighting vehicles swept through Tikrit before dawn, blasting with machine guns and heavy-weapons fire, houses that were suspected of being insurgent hideouts. (*Saskatchewan Peace News* vol. 11, November 2003). Compare the approach of the Indian army, which takes days to flush out just two or three terrorists trapped in a given location in order to minimize civilian casualties or collateral damage.

Iran, Saudi Arabia and Pakistan, the last named much later in the day after its military had been suitably used for other purposes. Hence, it is not difficult to see as to why the potential victims – just outlined – would not be taking the minimal steps to ensure that US comfort levels in Iraq do not reach the point that would enable the Americans to undertake further operations in their direction.

It must be added here that imperial powers throughout history have seldom, if ever, been dissuaded from their grand designs by temporary setbacks. Hence, a few years or even decades down the line the USA, after having sufficiently recovered from the Iraq misadventure – should it turn out to be so – would again set its sights towards accomplishing its global ambitions, albeit with the alterations necessitated by the passage of time. In like manner Islamic jehad is not likely to moderate its global ambitions either.

The Americans, for obvious reasons, do not like the situation in Iraq to be compared to that in Vietnam, several decades earlier. This is especially the case within the US establishment and the US military. Well-wishers of USA can understand as to why the comparisons would be odious to them. However, many people outside USA, who have been looking at the situation far more objectively, make the comparison from an entirely different angle. The differing view of external observers points not so much to the ignominious defeat or the pell-mell pullout by US forces from Vietnam, as to the handing over of the contested areas i.e. the whole of South Vietnam and later on Cambodia as well, as a result thereof, to their adversary, the North Vietnam regime. As is well known, the communist North Vietnam consolidated its hold comprehensively over both parts of Vietnam after the US was forced to quit.

Something similar could happen in Iraq. Should the Americans be obliged to quit at any stage *in extremis,* forces inimical to USA and to Western interests could take a stranglehold of large tracts of Iraq. In that case, they too would follow up with the same geo-strategic power play which was the basis for the Anglo-American intervention in Iraq i.e. using Iraq as a launch pad for further consolidation in the Middle East; possibly elsewhere as well. Hence, it would be seen that after temporarily pushing out the Islamic fundamentalists from large portions of Afghanistan, the US would seem to have given them a far more solid hold on Iraq, a country with potentially much greater resources than Afghanistan. The fundamentalist Islamists, should they consolidate their grip on Iraq after driving out the Americans, would become almost unstoppable, because they would have salvaged for the Muslim psyche, throughout the Middle East and beyond, a victory that would, in some minds be deemed to be comparable to the victories of Saladin the Magnificent over the crusaders many centuries earlier.

As perceived from Washington, no doubt the Americans are not likely to allow the situation to come to such a sorry pass. In which case, what other options would America have to retrieve the situation. Tragically, the lone superpower, the mightiest high-tech warrior on earth, in its enraged-bull state might end up by devastating Iraq, rather than handing it over to their hated opponents.

It becomes the right moment then to encapsulate a few salient aspects of the situation in Iraq as it obtains currently as a prelude to the discussion on Iran. In as far as it relates to the US Army in Iraq, the following aspects need to be further highlighted:

- With the increase in the number of attacks on the occupation forces, on the face of it at least, the hunter has become the hunted. In just a few months the US forces that could earlier roam about confidently over most parts of Iraqi territory are now confined to their ghetto-like fortresses. After each major attack one more ring of steel is added to the perimeter. The US forces remain hemmed in, physically as well as mentally. The psychological stresses that the young minds of US soldiery are undergoing in their formative years, assailed by the hatred of the unwelcoming populace and the increasing danger to their life and limb will create distress that could last longer than the stresses caused by the Vietnam War. No doubt the situation in Iraq is different; however, the phenomenon is nearly global as far as mounting anti-Americanism is concerned. When these soldiers get back into the mainstream of US civil society the stresses generated in Iraq and its after-effects will permeate more deeply into the latter's bloodstream than the physical effect of the fatalities suffered in Iraq.

- In Iraq as well as in Afghanistan, after the savage effects of the initial high-tech onslaught have died down, the local elements fighting the Americans have found ways to effectively neutralize the high-tech advantage of the latter.
- After winning the war in both countries and bringing down the governments that were in power before the attacks, in case the hunter has become the hunted, as appears to be the case, one of the biggest problems that the US forces and their allies face is the need for higher allocations of combat elements for safeguarding the bases and fixed assets of the occupying forces. It leaves less effective combat strength for offensive operations, whose extent and periodicity is thereby curtailed. It is a difficulty that is being faced by the occupation forces with no prospect of immediate relief in sight.

Taken together the points enumerated above indicate a passing of the initiative from one side to the other, or at least a perceptible shift. Should this trend not be reversed the occupation forces, over a period of time, could suffer losses that become unsustainable. At the very least, these would be difficult to justify in the countries that sent the forces against the protests of a large percentage of the population. Battling it out to the bitter end does not appear to serve any worthwhile purpose.

## Recapitulation of the situation in the Regional Context

In the regional context, the situation obtaining can be summarized as:

- Increasing hostility to American intervention in Iraq· was manifesting itself much before the blasts that struck Istanbul and stunned Turkey and the world in the third week of November 2003. Turkish peasants had already taken to stoning American military vehicles. The hostility, which began as opposition to American intervention could, if not checked turn into an all out hostility towards America. It has a bearing on Turkish membership of the EU.
- The stand off between USA and North Korea remains unresolved.
- More and more places around the world are becoming unsafe for US citizens. The Travel Warnings for its citizens issued by the US Department of State are increasing with each passing year.
- By encouraging suicide bombers based on religious indoctrination, Islamist fundamentalists could well be on their way to bringing collective retaliatory action from a world growing increasingly weary of suicide attacks on non-military targets and the mounting casualties to innocent people.

- Iran is light years away from posing a credible military threat to USA. If so inclined, it could in a decade or so pose a limited threat to US interests in Asia. Additionally, Iran as presently constituted and in the conditions obtaining in the region would be unlikely to harbour expansionist ambitions. Its rearmament would be limited to protection of its territory and its oil assets.
- Reestablishing security in Iraq could become the prime concern of the international community regardless of how the situation has come about.
- An English writer Jeremy Seabrook described the recent passage of President Bush through London as 'a funeral cortege'. (More on this later).
- 'Natofication' of Iraq. Proposal made by Bill Clinton recently in an interview given to Nayan Chanda might not be the answer. [2]
- European leaders who backed USA against the opinion of their people may lose their hold on power i.e. Silvio Berlusconi in Italy, Azhnar in Spain. The division between the Old and New Europe was artificially contrived through astute British diplomacy at the establishment levels of the countries that supported Anglo-American intervention in Iraq. As distinct from this, at the grassroots there was a near total opposition to the intervention throughout Europe.
- Conflicting loyalties could emerge in the Muslim populations residing in non-Muslim countries. (Already happening).
- Undue focus on US Presidential elections. The Iraq problem will not go away regardless of who wins the elections.

- Faking Iraq intelligence. Claims made by the global powers based on intelligence inputs would hereafter remain suspect.
- If one of the attributes of a superpower is extended global reach, then the only other entity that comes near to attaining that attribute is Islamist fundamentalism.
- The debate over the draconian powers that the US government has assumed in the war on terrorism, which includes the ongoing war in Iraq, could become more bitter.
- Civil liberties continue to be eroded around the world as a direct outcome of the threat posed by Islamic jehad. The latest in the series is the proposed special legislation, The Civil Contingencies Bill being considered by the British government. It is believed to be the biggest shake up of emergency laws since the early part of the last century, replacing a law that saw Britain through a World War and IRA bombing campaign. In some respects it goes further than the US Patriot Act.[3]
- The WTC bomber profile can serve as a false image, if applied across the board for future anticipatory actions. It need not represent the archetype in operations hereafter.
- As regards USA-Europe relations the following points merit attention: while Europe is generally at peace within and without, USA faces security challenges almost everywhere; the concept of indivisible US-Europe security is undergoing modification, far-reaching changes could take place in the not too distant future; there are distinct signs that Europe is striving for strategic autonomy from USA; Germany

is coming out of its 50 years plus self-restraint to find its feet as well as its voice as a political player on the European and global scene, again and again it has shown that as opposed to most other countries it cannot be dictated to or pushed. It did not give in when China created a furore over the Dalai Lama, nor did it give in to US blandishments over Iraq; Europe and USA have other fundamental divergences, e.g., over the Kyoto protocol and the International Criminal Court.

- For the present, the chances of Iraq under American occupation becoming like Afghanistan under Russians are remote. The opponents in Iraq, unlike those in Afghanistan, do not have a superpower to arm them. They do not have an equivalent of Pakistan from which to mount their attacks. Nor are they likely to acquire one: even those neighbours who may wish to see America fail in Iraq have an even stronger wish not to provoke that country into lashing out at them.[4]
- On the economic aid front, the European Union, which accounts for 20 percent of the world's wealth, offered only $250 million for Iraq. American officials were taken aback by what they viewed as a minuscule amount. But the political fact of life in Europe is that the Iraq war remains unpopular, and Bush himself is widely disliked.[5]
- Iraq is fast becoming the focal point of various types of radical Islamists and other groups fired by their anti-American zeal. Irrespective of improvement or deterioration in the ground situation no amount of troops that either USA or UN could muster can prevent these elements from infiltrating into or exfiltrating from Iraq on account of the large and porous frontiers. It means that these groups can come

in to take a devastating toll of US troops and their allies or they can simply come in to regroup and replenish themselves for exfiltrating in to Saudi Arabia or other Arab countries that they may wish to destabilize. The biggest worry will remain for the Saudi regime.

- Despite the rhetoric, the Syrian response to the Israeli air strike revealed in all its ugliness the Arab weakness. Most countries in the region are beholden to the US in one form or another. Egypt, the traditional leader, has been living on an annual American subvention of some $2 billion since the Camp David accords came to be implemented and cannot chart out its own course. Others have military protection agreements with the US and can pay only lip-sympathy to the Arab cause.[6]
- At a time of growing fundamentalist appeal, Syrian society remains perhaps the most secular and pluralistic among all the multi-religious states of the region.[7]
- The widespread suspicion remains among Muslims that Iraq is only part of a wider American plan to subvert the faith. The appointment to a senior post in America's anti-terror team of a general quoted as slurring Islam, along with the American administration's apparent approval of an Israeli air strike earlier in October (2003) against Syria, tends to reinforce such fears.
- The Anglo-American special relationship or entente that endured for a century or more dissolved in the aftermath of the intervention in Iraq. Tony Blair may still win another term, as may George Bush. They may still enjoy a deep personal bond. Notwithstanding these bonds, hardly any British

government would be in a position in future to ignore the public sentiment against war in the Middle East. Therefore, even if the Americans were to nurture ambitions for regime change or intervention in Iran in the manner that they did in Iraq they are not likely to receive British military support by way of physical participation in the invasion by British soldiers. Jeremy Seabrook in a recent article likened George W. Bush's passage through London to that of a funeral cortège. If public sentiment is anything to go by the special relationship is practically dead. In the face of unprecedented anger at the visit of the US President, George W. Bush was leading the funeral procession of the century old special relationship.

## The US Situation at the Beginning of 2004

Charles Krauthammer, in a recent article in *The New York Times,* urged Americans to face up to their 'responsibilities' as the 'undisputed masters of the world'.[8]

The US administrator in Iraq, L Paul Bremer was reduced to citing tiny Liechtenstein as an example of a country without an army when asked in a *TIME* magazine interview whether Iraq would not still need an effective army in order to provide national security and combat the threat of international terrorists, once the coalition hands over power. His precise reply:[9]

"They'll have an army. But that is not a necessary attribute of sovereignty. There are governments all over the world that don't have armies. Liechtenstein comes to mind."

The extrapolations quoted above from recent pronouncements indicate the differences in perception of the US predicament within and outside USA as well as the anxieties that seep through the statements. The type of thinking that started the US on its 'march to folly' (the title of a book by the well known author Barbara Tuchman) could propel it towards greater follies in the coming years. Because of its military and economic might the pain from misguided US policies spills over to other parts of the world as well.

## New US Vulnerabilities

Economic power is much more diffuse than at the end of World War II. The U.S. share of global product is about 25 percent, half the share it had in 1945. (By about 2010 it could reduce further).

The United States imports about 60 percent of its oil requirements, up from 30 to 40 percent during the 1970s.

The U.S. current account deficit or trade deficit is now immense – well over $400 billion in 2002, running at an annual rate of about $500 billion in 2003. In the 1970s, the United States ran both deficits and surpluses, both generally less than about $20 billion per year. Consistent trade deficits for more than two decades have turned the United States from the largest creditor to the largest debtor country in the world. To gain some perspective on an annual trade deficit rate of $500 billion, this is about equal to the entire annual Gross Domestic Product of India at current exchange rates. In a falling stock market, foreigners are less inclined to finance the huge trade deficits that are part of the continuing U.S. economic binge. The prospects for large inflows of European money to finance the U.S. trade deficit are murky, at best. Foreign investment has been declining, and so has the U.S. dollar. U.S. foreign debt is growing fast. US budget surpluses that emerged late in the 1990s have now disappeared in a sea of red ink. Gross US federal debt is now over $6 trillion, or about 60 percent of GDP, compared to fewer than one trillion dollars and about 33 percent of GDP in 1980, a considerable amount of this debt is held by foreigners.

Perhaps, most important, the euro has now emerged as a credible alternative, and hence a possible competitor, to the dollar. Earlier fears about its stability, when it was introduced as a unit of account in 1999 and quickly lost ground to the dollar, have dissipated. The euro rose in value by about 20 percent relative to the dollar in 2002. The euro-zone is comparable in economic size to the United States. And while Germany and France, the largest economies in the euro-zone, have had low economic growth both tend to run current account surpluses so that they do not need capital imports to sustain domestic consumption.[10]

"America is currently engaged in a bold experiment to bring democracy to the Middle East. As it does so, it needs to pay a little more attention to tending the flame of democracy back home".[11]

Seeing the difficult position in which the US finds itself, it might look at other options to retrieve the situation or to lessen the rigours of failed policies. One of the safer or saner options that the Americans could hardly have considered would be for the USA to swallow the bitter pill, so to say, and set course to sup with the devil. The devil in US eyes, in this case being Iran, which was the third leg of their infamous 'Axis of Evil'.

That is one way of looking at it i.e., being obliged to sup with the devil. However, were the US establishment to hold a less jaundiced view and take a fresh look, free from cherished myths about Iran, they would find it to be a fairly attractive proposition.

## What could happen should the US decide to Intervene Unilaterally in Iran

In the unlikely event of the USA attempting to intervene unilaterally in Iran, in the manner that it did in Iraq it would find its difficulties compounded by the following developments:

- The EU would act more stoutly to deflect US action;
- This time round a Tony Blair would not be able to engineer a split between what was referred to as Old and New Europe;
- The English public would not allow deployment of English troops in Iran to support an American offensive;
- France would not stand idly by;
- Germany would not allow the use of its bases for offensive action against Iran; similar action can be anticipated from several other European countries bowing to public pressure, possibly Turkey as well;
- Russia would not remain a passive bystander;
- Short of opposing the USA militarily, India would take all steps necessary to prevent the invasion of Iran;
- Rallying of global public opinion to deny access to US military vessels at ports of call around the world including, possibly, traditional allies like Australia, Canada and the UK;
- Condemnation in the UN and other international forums;
- Boycotting of US products;
- Many other actions of a similar nature that would make it clear to the US public that the world would not countenance further US unilateralism to invade countries that do not pose a direct threat to USA.

The tabulation above should bring home to the US public that their country would have to pay dearly for continued flouting of the UN Charter. In any case, as things stand the US would find the proposition to be militarily infeasible owing to overstretch and the deteriorating situation in Iraq. Iraq was supposed to have been the jump off point for US forces in the region for expansion in the chosen direction. It is no longer possible for USA to use it as a base for attacking Iran. Similarly, Afghanistan does not lend itself for an attack on Iran from that direction. Which leaves only Baluchistan in Pakistan as a military base for the attack on Iran. It is apparently being prepared for such contingencies.

The excerpts below give a clearer picture of the Russian perspective where it perceives a threat to its vital interests in Central Asia:

Russia's defence minister said that Moscow could use military force if its economic interests in vital regions of the world are not respected. "Force can be used when there is an attempt to limit Russia's access to vital regions of the world, including from an economic or financial point of view," the Interfax news agency quoted Sergei Ivanov as saying during a visit to Reykjavik, Iceland. Ivanov named two other cases in which force could be used: if there was a direct military threat against Russia or if instability in neighbouring former Soviet republics threatens Russians. Ivanov did not name a specific region in his remarks about economic access.[12]

Russian Defence Minister Sergei Ivanov stated that Russia retained the right to launch pre-emptive military strikes to protect its interests, but he said nuclear weapons would not be used in any such attack. Ivanov did not rule out the use of nuclear weapons altogether, however. He told reporters that Russia would not hesitate to use them "If all other means are exhausted and we have no other way out. We are not going to give that up."[13]

Reference to pre-emptive use of force is a new element in Russia's defence strategy that was absent from the military doctrine adopted in 2000. It sends a clear warning to the U.S. to accept Russia's dominant role in the former Soviet states. The U.S. intrusion into Russia's traditional turf worries Moscow more and more. What began as temporary American military presence in Central Asia endorsed by Russia to facilitate the anti-terror war in Afghanistan, far from winding up, is expanding. In addition to airbases in Uzbekistan and Kyrgyzstan, the U.S. is helping Kazakhstan set up a naval base on the Caspian Sea close to the Russian border and is seeking to lease three military bases in Tajikistan. In Central Asia Washington conducts regular war games with Kazakhstan, Uzbekistan and Kyrgyzstan under NATO's Partnership for Peace programme and has launched officer training programmes for Tajikistan and Kyrgyzstan.

"We are against this policy (of pre-emptive strikes without the U.N. approval). But if this practice continues to be asserted in international relations, Russia retains the right to act in the same way," the Russian President, Vladimir Putin, said in an interview to Al-Jazeera TV.

Speaking at the presentation of the defence paper, Mr. Putin announced the impending deployment of "dozens" of the Soviet era's most powerful missiles, the SS-19 "Stiletto" armed with six nuclear warheads each. The mothballed missiles would be put on duty to phase out the aged missiles and would remain in service till the mid-2030s.

"Their capability to overcome any anti-missile defence is unrivalled," the Russian leader stressed. Russia is also developing a "fundamentally new missile system", which will take 10 to 15 years to build, according to the Strategic Rocket Forces Commander, General Nikolai Solovtsov.

For the first time since the collapse of the Soviet Union, Russia has projected a global role for its armed forces as "the factor in preventing the final collapse of the system of international relations based on international law. "It is the Armed Forces of the Russian Federation that can ensure global stability in the broader sense of this term."[14]

## Co-Opting Iran for Stability in the Middle East

The earlier part of the discussion centred around the need to prevent a unilateral US or Anglo-US intervention in Iran to bring about what is euphemistically referred to as a regime change, whatever the deeper motivation behind the intervention. It was seen that such a step has become unlikely in the foreseeable future owing to the US predicament in Iraq and Afghanistan – a clear case of over-extension. Proceeding on the basis that the inadvisability of such a step would have become apparent even to the leading votaries of an intervention in Iran, it might be worthwhile examining the possibility of co-opting Iran as the center point of stability in West Asia, even Central Asia. Appreciating that the Americans and some others might be astounded at such a turn of events, the question that would be foremost in everyone's mind would be 'Why Iran?'

## Why Iran?

Taking a fresh look at the possibility of co-opting Iran as the center point of West and Central Asian stability, free of past misgivings, prejudices or bitterness, the main considerations would encompass inter alia:

- The stability of the Iranian state when juxtaposed against the current or potential instability of the vast majority of its Islamic neighbours;
- Its central location, both from the point of view of current or projected hydrocarbon exports from the

region as well as the geographical location vis-à-vis the trouble spots of Iraq and Afghanistan and even Pakistan should the last-named country not be able to curb the export of terror at some future point in time.

- Iran's help could prove invaluable in stabilizing the situation in Afghanistan and would become crucial for Iraq's stabilization.
- Last, but not least, Iran with its great civilization and cultural tradition could become the harbinger of a responsible and liberal Muslim society at the heart of the so-called Crescent of Islam.

## What the Global Community would Expect of Iran

For such a situation to come about the global community, or more importantly the Western world, if it were to shed its past misgivings would at a minimum expect the following conditions to obtain:

- Total renunciation by Iran of its nuclear ambitions;
- Loosening of the hold of the ruling clergy and greater democratization with attendant freedom of the citizens and the press;
- Acceptance of the right of Israel to exist as a state;
- Cutting off of support to militant groups that draw or drew sustenance from Iran;
- Other liberalization measures;
- Integration into the global effort for the restoration of peace in the region to a degree that there would be no suspicion of the furtherance of its own agenda in any of the neighbouring states that could cause anxiety to the others.

## What Iran Could Expect in Return (from the Global Community)

In return for abjuring its nuclear ambitions and full-scale integration into the global community, the Iranian state could reasonably expect the following from the Western world:

- Non-interference in Iranian affairs;
- Lifting of all restrictions against Iran;
- Allowing Iran to compete fairly for the energy outflow from Central Asia via Iran;
- Access to nuclear technologies for peaceful uses;
- Investments in Iran and access to capital on liberal terms.

## Looking beyond Afghanistan-Iraq and the other Countries in the Region

More than the Islamists – they can be given any name i.e. Al-Qaeda, Taliban or the products of the *deeni madaris* of Pakistan – it is the Americans who now appear to be fighting with their backs to the wall. Today, the US stands more isolated than the Islamists who still enjoy tacit if not overt support in large parts of the Muslim world. America is the most criticized nation in the world. Most of its allies have distanced themselves from America in its Iraq misadventure. Americans cannot travel freely in many parts of the world. And so on. Whichever way one looks at it, the Americans seem to have painted themselves into a corner. They have also pulled down their mental shutters. Any further criticism, well-intentioned or otherwise, from friend or foe, is hardly welcome. Largely, it is water off a duck's back.

At the beginning of 2004 further criticism of the USA could become counter productive. Should the situation deteriorate more rapidly for USA in Iraq or in Afghanistan the repercussions would be felt not only in USA, but in the rest of the world as well. Therefore, the world needs to engage with USA – with the establishment as well as the civil society – to make the lone superpower change course for ushering in a more humane and rational world order. Should it alter course in the direction indicated, it can resume its leadership role for the best part of the century, and beyond. The world would willingly follow America were the nation to return to its true liberal values, rather than the distorted perspective that currently obtains.

## End Notes

1. *The Economic Times*, 6 October 2003.
2. Editor, *Yale Global Online*, reproduced in *The Statesman*, 23 November 2003.
3. *The Statesman*, World Focus, 25 November 2003.
4. *The Economist*, 23 August 2003.
5. *The New York Times*, reproduced in *International Herald Tribune*, 19 September 2003.
6. *The Tribune*, 14 October 2003, 'Weak response to Israeli attack' by S. Nihal Singh.
7. *The Indian Express*, 29 October 2003. 'Bush's rocky road to Damascus' by Raghav Gupta.
8. Sir Shridath Ramphal quoting an ideologue from the "regressive right", *Hindustan Times*, 22 November 2003.
9. As quoted in *TIME*, 24 November 2003.
10. Source *SCIENCE FOR DEMOCRATIC ACTION*, vol. 11; no. 3; June 2003.
11. *The Economist*, 16 August 2003.
12. *The Statesman*, 6 October 2003.
13. *USA Today*, Colorado Springs, reproduced in *The Hindustan Times*, 11 October 2003.
14. *The Hindu*, 4 November 2003, 'Russia flexes its muscles' by Vladimir Radyuhin.

# 5

## *Resurgence of Russia in the 21st Century[1]

"The dreams we shared did not come true...what seemed simple to us turned out to be tormentingly difficult". **

"He who does not regret the passing of socialism has no heart, but he who wants to bring it back has no head". ***

If historical experience is anything to go by then the speed and manner of disintegration of the Soviet Union (or the Russian Empire so to say) has no parallels. It was unique in more ways than one. Great empires of yore broke up on the death of a great leader, on account of external invasions, internal strife or the pushing back of the Empire from without. None of these factors could strictly be applied to the dismantling of the Soviet Empire. The outside world—

---

* Based on talk delivered at the United Service Institution, New Delhi on 10 January 2001; repeated at Orlando, USA at the end of January 2001.

** Boris Yeltsin's lament while departing.

*** Vladimir Putin summing up his philosophy not long after he was elected, in a phrase that has become famous throughout Russia.

as well as the Republics comprising the Soviet Union—were both taken by surprise at the bewildering speed of events that led to the break up. Remarkably, many of the non-Russian republics were initially reluctant to face the prospects of life outside the Soviet fold.

By hindsight there appears to have been an inevitability about the outcome though not its pace. The former can be attributed to the abating vigour of a once ascendant ideology in the face of the relentless onslaught of capitalism at its naked best—or worst, for those inclined to look at it that way. The Soviet Union did not collapse due to external aggression or unmanageable internal strife. On the face of it, it was relatively as stable as any large, heterogeneous entity can hope to be in this day and age. Economic collapse and loss of faith in the system—again more perhaps at the centre rather than the periphery—helped the disembodiment.

The counter-revolution could be deemed to have commenced from the time that Mikhail Gorbachev, Secretary-General of the Communist Party, ushered in the new age of *glasnost* (openness) and *perestroika* (reconstruction). Somewhere along the way he lost control of the process, which led ultimately to the dissolution of the Soviet Union and the emergence of the Russian Federation, as part of the Commonwealth of Independent States in December 1991. Gorbachev was not spared either. He fell by the wayside as elements more powerful than him moved in to exploit the situation.

The post-collapse phase of the Soviet Union also seems to be coming to an end. According to Yevgeny Kozhokin: "Today, we are witnessing a gradual ideological recreation of Russia. The Soviet past and the Russian past and present are less frequently confronted, but are accepted and evaluated as parts of the whole".[2]

This paper relates to the Resurgence of Russia. Naturally, there would be doubt in some quarters as to whether Russia could again attain superpower status. While this aspect will be examined at some length it might not be out of place, at the very outset, to spell out some of the major attributes of a superpower in the new century. Briefly, these could be tabulated as: ability for (rapid) force projection anywhere in the world; credible second-strike capability against all comers; financial might; technical might; and last, but not least, the intellectual vigour of its academic institutions. By these criteria hardly any country beside the USA could be said to be in the superpower category not only as things stand, but in the foreseeable future as well.

There could be several ways of looking at the subject under review. The method chosen in this presentation examines the issue from the following perspectives:

- Conditions in Russia
- The Demographic Dynamic
- Russia 'in' Asia
- Russia 'in' Europe
- Russia and USA
- Concluding Remarks

There would be many more aspects that cry for inclusion in a longer narrative. These have perforce to be excluded in a short presentation.

## Conditions in Russia

The Russian Federation sprawls over 17 million square kilometers in Europe and Asia. Notwithstanding its geographical spread the once powerful country today merits a place only at number 71 out of the 174 countries on the UN's Human Development Index which lists countries according to literacy, life expectancy, schooling, population growth and per capita GDP. The average life expectancy of Russian men is 59, fourteen years less than their counterparts in the West—a reflection of poor living conditions and widespread alcoholism. By current trends the Russian population will decline from 146 million to 124 million by 2015. Russia needs hard cash from swift arms sales, even throwing caution to the winds in some cases.

It would be tempting, hence, to assume that the end of the twentieth century marks the lowest point in the falling trajectory of Russia's gradual rise to superpowerhood since the Russian expansion under Peter the Great nearly three centuries ago. But the realisation comes soon thereafter that Russia had stared at the abyss before; in the same century, at the very beginning. Conditions for Russia could hardly have been grimmer than at the time when Lenin took power. The country not only recovered, but went on to challenge, thereafter, the combined might of the Western powers for the best part of the century. It would indeed be a foolhardy person who would feel emboldened to write *finis* to the Russian tale.

Already there are tentative signs of revival. GDP has risen since 1999, although in part due to high oil prices. The State Duma on 8 December 2000 endorsed the old Soviet anthem proposed by Yeltsin's successor. Putin balanced the anthem choice with the tricolour flag and the double-headed eagle, which date from the tsarist times and were reintroduced by Yeltsin. Both symbols were also approved by the Parliament. Putin justified the proposal by saying that he hoped the state symbols belonging to different periods of Russian history would cement the nation. Russian liberals protested against the Soviet anthem as a tune of the totalitarian regime that had been personally approved by the Communist dictator, Josef Stalin. Many read symbolic meaning into the revival of the Soviet anthem on 8 December, ten years to the day after Yeltsin dismantled the Soviet Empire.

Russian resurgence, however, cannot really take place without the satisfactory resolution of the major problems confronting Russia. These include: population decline; ecological restoration; tackling Islamic terrorism; revitalisation of the economy; better harmonisation with the republics of the erstwhile USSR; strengthening of ties with Europe; dealing with the demographic swamping that could manifest itself from the south.

Not long back—merely three decades ago—the other superpower USA suffered a major setback in Vietnam. It was an ignominious defeat for American arms. Along with the debacle in Southeast Asia came the demoralisation of the American armed forces, especially the army. Indiscipline, corruption and drugs added to the problem. The US army pulled itself up by the bootstraps. Not only did they recover, the US armed forces are once again in the forefront. It is to be seen whether the demoralisation that set in the Russian troops after the pullback from Afghanistan and continues with the imbroglio in Chechnya can be overcome before the country plunges into an existential gloom.

One of the factors that could play a major role in any reversal would be the leadership provided by Yeltsin's successor. The Russian Federation's Foreign Policy Concept issued on 11 July 2000 reaffirms its determination to pursue a balanced foreign policy between the East and West and seeks closer co-operation with major Asian countries like China and India. Presently, Russia is in a state of adjustment. The real policy thrusts indicating the final course adopted by Russia will emerge by about 2005 *after* Putin has been at the head for at least that length of time. Mid-term corrections would, of course, continue.

## Vladimir Vladimirovich Putin

Russia bespeaks vastness, on a scale unknown elsewhere in the world. In keeping with this bigness its leaders too assume a dimension commensurate with the country's size. The word 'great' comes naturally to mind. Not necessarily in the manner of the honorific bestowed on some of the past rulers by posterity, Peter the Great, Catherine the Great. In the 20th century, Lenin and Stalin not only dominated their country absolutely, they projected Russian communism onto the global canvas. Even Yeltsin was not insignificant as a leader—though possibly in the negative sense—seeing his contribution to the rapid downslide of a once proud people. He did not comprehend the survival imperative entailed in the near-total dependence on social security of a populace that had been living under a communist dispensation for the best part of a century. It is not easy to switch overnight from one system to another without horrendous social costs, leading even to the ebbing of the will to live, the will to work. It has lessons for China and India, both of whom seem bent upon succumbing to external pressures to take the fast track to globalisation. The last decade has been economically devastating for Russia. According to some estimates, there are 50 million Russians below the poverty line, 20 million fully or partially unemployed. Ten million refugees are homeless.

The Yeltsin era accentuated Russia's intrinsic weaknesses: vodka, environmental decline, demographic enfeeblement and ethnic dissension. The rapid post-Soviet decline, the excesses of the past, and the Yeltsin years saw the diminishment of the country's global standing to such an extent that the world took serious note of Russia solely on account of the nuclear equation as a means to power projection. It led in turn to the drying up of future leading edge research, due to financial stringency and the initial flight of scientific talent.

The Russian people expect that President Putin would be able to curb the free-for-all nature of post-Soviet politics, discipline the new capitalist brigands who have accumulated unacceptable levels of power and wealth, and impose what he calls a dictatorship of laws on Russia. There is a growing feeling among the people that the darkest period could be behind them. A report by the consulting firm, McKinsey, mentioned that Russia has the real and human capital for a growth rate of 8 percent. Barely two years ago, the Russian economy was in ruins. It had defaulted on its foreign loans, and inflation had risen from 5.5 percent in the first half of the year (1998) to 84 percent in December. Moscow's control over its 89 regions was slipping. But since then Russia has experienced a turnaround. Many in Russia feel that the years 1992 to 1999 are beginning to fade like a bad dream. Most wage arrears have reportedly been paid off. Real incomes are rising and possibly the pensions as well. There appears to have been an improvement in the investment outlook, with some companies reporting plans to expand investment in the coming years.

Having quoted from the McKinsey study, it would be worthwhile to look at global oil trends because of Russia's over-dependence on the oil revenues. Without the rise in oil prices the rosy tint of the report may have had a different colouring. A comparison that comes to mind was the 'unprecedented prosperity and social stability' in the 1970s, attributed by some to the Middle East crisis and the formation of OPEC in 1973. It is worth reproducing here an extract from an article by Valentina Feodorova:

"Russia tends to be radical. This is its main disease. We chose the most radical—communist—of all-possible variants of socialism. We also chose the most radical, neo-liberal, variant of capitalism, which is a kind of Western fundamentalism. The political pendulum of Russia moved from communist radicalism to a neo-liberal one. We could expect it to move back, for this is what pendulums do. But a part of the older and the bulk of the middle-aged generations that experienced both variants are not ready for extremes today. They preferred Putin to Zyuganov at the 2000 elections. The people want to live in the new way, but in conditions of order. The pendulum has stopped a little left of the centre, but not in the far left corner. That Putin has kept back the movement of the pendulum is the main and new factor of Russian politics".[3]

Putin is very much a product of the Marxist ideology that flourished so long in Russia. Hence, it might not be out of place to quote Georgy Lukacs on Lenin: "The Leninist theory and tactic of compromise is, therefore, only the objective, logical corollary of the Marxist dialectical-historical recognition that, although men make their own history, they cannot do so in circumstances chosen by themselves but in circumstances directly encountered, given and transmitted from the past".[4]

The Russian leader has been moving fast to tighten his grip on power. He has pushed through legislation to remove powerful regional governors from the upper house of Parliament and turn it into a subservient instrument of his policy. He is also attempting to rein in Russia's freewheeling regions by taking away from them control over courts and law-enforcement agencies. The same zealousness is manifest in his control of television that is by far the most influential source of information in a country that spans 11 time zones. The Putin dispensation has spelled out its security and foreign policy doctrines. Moscow recognises that many of its security challenges are internal, acknowledging in the process that its economic difficulties have led to terrorism, organised crime and narcotics. Putin believes that the entire Central Asian Region could be destabilised if the Taliban again reach the Tajikistan border. On the economic front realisation may have come that for global competitiveness Russia needs to revive its capital goods base. In this regard Europe and especially Germany could play a big role. Good governance could help in ensuring return of capital stashed abroad.

The world and, more importantly, the Russian people themselves would be anxious to take a peek behind the KGB-like mask for there is a mystery and mystique attaching to the persona of the Russian President. Is it greater than the substance? The judo black belt does add to the carefully nurtured strong and silent macho image. It assists in a manner of speaking to reinforce the arm-twisting being resorted to bring a semblance of order into the free-for-all that had developed in the Yeltsin years. However, the Russian leader lest he again provide legitimacy to the earlier methods of governance in the Soviet Union should keep in mind a saying attributed to Talleyrand: 'It is possible' he said, 'to do many things with a bayonet, but one cannot sit on one.'

## The Demographic Dynamic

As distinct from India, which suffers from a so-called population explosion, Russia is beset by what might be described as a demographic implosion — that is there are fewer and fewer of them every year. Over the past decade the population of Russia has shrunk by nearly 5 million people, or half a million annually. Not only has the vast country got fewer people, the balance between young and old is shifting disastrously. In the coming years there will be only two working age Russians for each pensioner and within 20 years the ratio will become one-to-one, the point of economic non-viability would have been reached. The growing mass of pensioners will gobble up any economic growth.

The demographic crisis has come about because post-Soviet Russia in many ways is afflicted with many problems of the advanced countries combined with growing problems that beset developing countries. For over two decades birthrates have been plunging as well-educated, urbanised young Russians put off having children well into their 30s. The current birth rate is about 1.3 children per woman, well below the 2.3 children per woman that would be required to sustain the population—a phenomenon not unlike that in Western Europe and North America. The difference being that over the past decade death rates among productive adults in their 30s and 40s have risen dramatically. This is due to a post-Soviet mix of bad news, including mass impoverishment, deteriorating environmental conditions, skyrocketing rates of alcoholism, the return of formerly-eradicated diseases like cholera and tuberculosis, more industrial accidents and bloody civil wars against the separatist republic of Chechnya.

President Putin has warned that if the Far Eastern region is not economically developed and integrated with the rest of the country, then it is likely that Chinese, Japanese and Korean languages may overtake the Russian language there. Maritime province governor, Yevgeny Nazdarenko made a call for moving about 15 million people from the Central regions to be settled in Amur, Khabarovsk and Primorsky (Maritime) areas in order to create some balance with the population in the adjoining Chinese regions.

The extract reproduced from a famous book written at the beginning of the twentieth century does not leave room for doubt:

"In those (coming) days all the people of the earth will rush forth from their dwelling places. Great will be the strife, strife the like of which has never been seen in this world. The yellow hordes of Asians will set forth from their age-old abodes and will encrimson the fields of Europe in oceans of blood. There will be, oh yes, there will— Tsushima! There will be-a new Kalka!

Kulikovo Field, I await you!

And on that day the final sun will rise in radiance over my native land. Oh Sun, if you do not rise, then, oh Sun, the shores of Europe will sink beneath the heavy Mongol heel, and the foam will curl over those shores. Earthborn creatures once more will sink to the depths of the oceans, into chaos, primordial and long-forgotten.

Arise, oh Sun!" [5]

It is estimated that vast numbers of Chinese settlers could already have pushed across the far-eastern border with Russia and the erstwhile Soviet republic of Kazakhstan. The exodus commenced after the break up of the Soviet Union on account of the sparseness of the population and to meet the requirement of cheap labour. What the population profile would be in that part of Russia in thirty, fifty or seventy years from now could be anybody's guess. The demographic threat from the south, linked to Islamic terrorism could ultimately become a bigger disaster for Russia than any threat faced by the country in the last century. The urge for quick economic gains is making the Russian planners abandon prudence by supplying the most modern technology to those who would be likely to develop into the most potent threat for Russia in the coming decades.

## Russia 'in' Asia

To begin with it would be interesting to list the countries that were the greatest beneficiaries of the fall of the Soviet Union: USA, East Europe, Western European countries,

China, Pakistan, (in that order). Central Asian Republics? The question mark denotes a Yes-No condition. It is important to keep this aspect at the back of the mind. It is not only relevant to Russia's strategic posture in the short and medium term, but also for the *inter se* accommodations that might or might not take place as Russia again starts groping for a more balanced relationship with yesterday's adversaries as well as the potential adversaries of tomorrow.

Russia as is well known straddles both continents, Asia and Europe. Till Peter the Great turned his attention westwards and forced the Westernisation of his country, Russia could be said to have been more deeply involved with Asia than Europe for more reasons than one. It was this attraction for the Orient that prompted Dostoievski to say in the latter half of the nineteenth century:

"Give us Asia and we shall create no difficulties for Europe"

The novelist also said: "It would be useful for Russia to forget Petersburg for some time and to turn her soul toward the East". [6]

With this background it is intended to examine Russia's relationship with some of the countries in Asia that could be deemed to be important for Russia geopolitically in the foreseeable future. Due to several constraints only those aspects will be highlighted that in the writer's opinion have a direct bearing on the subject under review.

## Russia and China

In the past, the former Soviet Union had a 7,500 km border with China (in comparison India's frontier with China after the latter's occupation of Tibet measures 4,700 km. Together they constituted 80 percent of China's external borders). Today Russia's borders have come down to 4,300 km, less than that of China and India. The Russian/Soviet border with China was determined by the Treaty of Aigun (1858); the Treaty of Peking 1860; the Treaty of St. Petersburg 1881; and subsequent borders protocols. However, the Chinese regarded only the much earlier 1689 Treaty of Nerchinsk as equal, which placed Russia's border in the Far East as far north as the Sea of Okhotsk.

There has been talk of a Russia-China-India axis. It does not appear to be feasible unless three conditions obtain from the point of view of Russia. The first condition would be for Russia to become as economically strong as China. Secondly, the demographic threat from China should have virtually disappeared from the horizon—a near impossibility going by the present demographic trends obtaining in the region. The third aspect relates to the maintenance of technical and qualitative superiority in the very advanced weapons systems category. The situation could change fast for the worse should Russia continue to throw caution to the winds by transferring advanced technologies to China for short-term gains. China has been ably tapping the cash-and-carry opportunities in the Russian market, picking up a number of sensitive technologies. (Even the United States was quick to buy advanced Russian space and rocket technologies cheaply in the early nineties). Ironically, because of these transfers and sales China might end up replacing Russia as the second power sometime in the future. At the moment there is talk of multi-polarity. In actual fact multi-polarity is a staging point towards just two poles; that could re-emerge after China has narrowed the military technology gap with USA—with Russian help, so to say. Then the relationship will subtly change. That will be the stage when Russia starts crying over spilt milk.

China aspires to superpower status at par with USA at some point in time. This is unlikely to happen unless China is able to marginalise Russia and Japan and to a lesser extent India. All these countries have geographic contiguity with China. In the case of Japan, the sea between China and Japan makes them contiguous. All three nations have the potential to challenge China in various fields. Their respective spheres of economic and geopolitical influence in and around the region impinge upon each other. Recent efforts by the Russian leader to establish a more direct relationship with North Korea and the Koreas in general could conceivably make China uncomfortable. Japan and the two Koreas would look at the development differently, perhaps more benignly. Additionally, China will emerge as a world power only after it has been able to incorporate Taiwan. Lee Kuan Yew the elder statesman of Singapore put it succinctly in an interview: "If China does not disintegrate reunification is inevitable. If China disintegrates all bets are off". [7]

## Russia and Iran

Russia apparently is quietly building a strategic relationship with Iran. Russia has made an agreement with Iran to supply about 4 billion US dollars worth of material in the next few years to the Iranian armed forces. These include: military aircraft, tanks, air defence systems and diesel submarines. In early February 2000 Russia turned down an offer of $100 million in aid from the US Department of Energy if it promised to end the reprocessing of nuclear fuel and cancel the Bushehr project.[8] The Bushehr project would give a much-needed boost to Russian industry. It is estimated at US$ 800 million.

At one point the US seemed to be persisting with its efforts to prevent Russia, China and Iran from coming closer in any combination between these countries. The Russia-China-Iran axis cannot really emerge as a durable axis for more reasons than one. It was developing primarily on account of the feeling in Iran and Russia that they were being pushed into a corner by the Americans. Should the moderates in Iran led by President Khatami succeed in their thrust towards liberalisation and should the US, in turn, moderate its stance the outcome could turn out differently. Initially, the US strategic goal of total control of Central Asian gas and oil aimed at excluding Russia and Iran by any combination that would sidestep these countries. At that point the Afghan-Pakistan corridor was being looked at favourably.

Major changes have taken place since then. China's geo-strategic planning now aims—in the long-term, if not immediately—at being the dominant power in Central Asia. The early occupation of Tibet—and now an enfeebled Russia—will permit China to do so through physical dominance of the region, directly or by proxy. That proxy certainly cannot be Iran. It is the Pakistan-Afghanistan axis that China seeks to exploit to the hilt in the coming years to checkmate the other major powers having interests in the region.

Iran's efforts to stem the Taliban tide were impelled by geo-strategic and ideological imperatives. Russia too must feel uncomfortable at China's backing Pakistan with such vigour, and by extension the Taliban, with nuclear and longer-range missile technologies. While ostensibly these transfers were meant to keep India engaged, strategic thinkers in Russia, Turkey and Israel reportedly started feeling uncomfortable at the thought that they too could become vulnerable to the same weapons systems under a more militant Islamic dispensation.

## Russia and Central Asian Republics

On taking over as President of the Russian Federation, Putin began to play a more active role in the sphere of foreign policy. In May 2000, he had meetings with most of the Commonwealth of Independent States (CIS) leaders. Russia desisted from setting forth any global or ideological agenda in the manner of a superpower. The new concept was one of multipolar system of international relations, which objectively reflected the reality at the dawn of the new century.

Russia then embarked on a sweeping reshaping of its relations with the former Soviet states, abandoning attempts to resuscitate the CIS and preferring instead to build alliances with its closest allies on the basis of shared interests. The new strategy could aggravate splits in the CIS. On the other hand, it could start economic integration among at least some of the CIS members.

Meeting in Astana, the capital of Kazakhstan in October 2000 the Presidents of Russia, Kazakhstan, Kyrgyzstan, Tajikistan and Belarus, set up a new economic trade zone, the Eurasian Economic Community. The five countries agreed to gradually pull down economic barriers and encourage free movement of goods, capital and workforce. Russia showed willingness to put up with certain economic losses resulting from the opening of the domestic market to its partners. Moscow also forfeited the right to dominate the grouping, although it will control 40 percent of the votes in the new union.

Soon after they formed the Eurasian Economic Community the five former Soviet states, joined by Armenia, met in Bishkek, capital of Kyrgyzstan, to resuscitate the 1992 Collective Security Treaty. The six nations resolved to set up a rapid deployment military force to repulse both external aggression and internal insurgency. What is more important, Moscow agreed to supply weapons to its allies at highly concessional rates.

Since the breakup of the Soviet Union in 1991 Ukraine had been drifting away from Russia and opposed any CIS accords that could hamper this process. In 1999, Ukraine set up a NATO-oriented security arrangement with Georgia,

Uzbekistan, Azerbaijan, which refused to prolong the Collective Security Treaty with Russia, as well as Moldova. The new alliance, GUUAM, which drew its abbreviation from the first letter of its member-states' names, was formally established in Washington in May 1999 where its leaders attended celebrations of the 50th anniversary of NATO. From the start it favoured closer economic, political and military co-operation with the West.

The establishment of the Eurasian Economic Community and rekindling of the Collective Security Treaty highlighted the split in the CIS into pro-Russia and pro-NATO camps. The President of Uzbekistan, Mr. Islam Karimov, refused to attend the Moscow-led summits in Kazakhstan and Kyrgyzstan and played host instead to the Ukrainian President. At about the same time Russia's Lukoil pulled out of a consortium of Western-led companies that were planning to build oil and gas pipelines from Azerbaijan to Turkey. The Russian natural gas monopoly, Gazprom, drew up plans to build a pipeline to Europe bypassing Ukraine. This would cost Ukraine many millions of dollars in lost gas transit revenues. Oil politics continue to dominate the region. The European and US investments in Central Asia have grown substantially in the past decade. However, due to its geographic location and linguistic affinities, Russia is better placed to assist existing regimes in matters of defence and internal order.

An important indicator of changing attitudes towards Russia in the region is the position of President Karimov of Uzbekistan. In 1999 Karimov distanced himself from the CIS by becoming a member of the NATO-sponsored GUUAM Pact, which united former Soviet southern republics in a loose alliance. He also refused to sign the CIS defence pact. Following major terrorist activity in his territory, however and an attempt on his life, Karimov sought greater co-operation with Russia in dealing with fundamentalist organisations. While stressing the need to build up Uzbek military forces, he agreed to send Uzbek officers for training at the military academy of the Russian Federation, and ensured refurbishing of Uzbek hardware from Russia. Russia cannot really shed its Soviet legacy. It cannot opt out unilaterally. If it does, the vacuum created in the CAR would, in all probability, be filled by forces inimical to Russia. Putin's quandary is that he cannot afford to leave them alone.

## Russia and Afghanistan

The US was able to get out of Vietnam after the defeat at the hands of the Vietcong, practically abandoning all military and non-military assets *in situ*. Whatever the mess, it turned out to be a 'clean break'. No such luxury was available to Russia on account of geographical contiguity and a host of other factors that have already been touched upon earlier on in the paper. Russia remained in the forefront of the global efforts to contain the Taliban and the potential for terrorism emanating from that country.

Russia really does not have much of a choice in the matter. Either it is successful in containing the militant Islamic threat or it watches as more and more regions in Central Asia and Russia itself go the Chechnya way. The dilemma is very real. It has been amply demonstrated in Vietnam and Afghanistan that advanced military technology in itself while it can flatten a country and destroy its infrastructure by the use of aircraft and missiles cannot adequately deal with small, well-motivated guerrilla bands. More so, in mountainous and jungle terrain, should capture of territory be the real objective. Radical groups bent upon mayhem require well-trained troops to flush them out in close quarter combat, where body count matters. Casualties (in men) can be high. This is where Russia has to take a firm decision since it cannot afford to expend manpower. The strategy of the opponents is to make the battle manpower heavy, which hurts Russia with a declining population much more than it does the adversary. The Russians cannot sustain more and more manpower losses. Therefore, that country would be left with no option but to strike at source by delineating a line, which if breached by the jehadis in Afghanistan, or their backers, would automatically invite massive high tech precision retaliation. The retaliation would be limited to training camps and such assets that allow the other side to pursue its northward thrust into the CAR.

## Russia and Japan

The defence relationship between Japan and Russia is likely to grow, driven by a wariness of China. This could be greatly strengthened by increased economic co-operation. Raw fossil fuels and the resources locked up in the coldness of Siberia have long beckoned Japan's hungry industry. Japanese businessmen continue to show reluctance on account of the complicated political relations between the two countries. Japan is anxious to see tangible progress towards the return of the four islands known to the world as the Kuriles: more precisely the islands of Shikotan, the Habomai cluster, Kunashiri and Etorofu. In 1855, towards the end of the Tokugawa Shogunate, Japan and Russia signed a Treaty of friendship, drawing a border between the northernmost of the four islands, Etorofu, and Russia's Urup Island. During the period leading to the Japanese surrender in September 1945, the Soviets grabbed all four islands. In 1956, during the establishment of diplomatic relations, Japan and Russia signed the Moscow Declaration. It calls for Russia returning Habomai and Shikotan when the peace treaty is signed. The fate of the other two islands was not mentioned.

After many ups and downs Japan coaxed Russia in 1993 to again formally acknowledge the existence of a territorial dispute. Later, during the Hashimoto visit to Russia, he mooted the idea of 'land for money'. Japan would invest in infrastructure in the Russian Far East and could buy natural gas at cheaper prices, and improve Russia's ports, harbours and other facilities on the disputed islands. In return, Mr. Yeltsin agreed to sign a document saying both leaders would do their best in order to conclude a peace treaty by 2000. There were further talks during Mr. Yeltsin's visit to Japan in 1998. In spite of all the parleys there really has not been any satisfactory forward movement in this issue from the Japanese viewpoint.

In the coming years these countries will have to shed their past antipathy and take a fresh look at the emerging geopolitical scene in Asia and the world. Both countries are global players. They might have to make fresh assessments about their global role. Although the possibility may appear remote at the moment, China through tacit support to the Pakistan-Taliban axis as well as its direct investments in Kazakhstan, especially in the oil sector, is getting poised to dominate the Central Asian region at some future date. They have already consolidated their hold over Tibet. Neither Japan nor Russia would view this development with equanimity. For both countries, China appears to be the bigger worry in the future rather than any misgivings about each other.

## Russia and India

The Russian relationship with India would be seen by many as a near perfect relationship on account of the absence of dissonance on almost any count, be it trade, geopolitical interests or any other sphere that is included in relations between countries. Not being geographically contiguous cross border irritants also get excluded. To add to this, at the present time both countries are threatened by militant Islamic groups sallying forth from the Afghanistan-Pakistan region. There appears to be a national consensus in both countries on closer co-operation. To quote Professor Sergei Lunyov, a leading specialist at the Institute of Oriental Studies:

"We must never forget that Russia and India are natural geopolitical allies. There is a lot of momentum in the relationship."

The Russian proposal for a North-South Transport Corridor on establishing a railroad-cum-ferry link between Russia and India through several other countries has been well received. The Indian Transport Minister signed an agreement in St Petersburg pledging Indian co-operation in implementing the project, estimated to cost nearly $2 billion. It will cut delivery time from India to Russia by 10 to 15 days and save about 30 percent in shipping costs. Originating in Helsinki and proceeding via St Petersburg, Moscow, Astrakhan, the Caspian Sea, Iran, UAE to India – the Corridor will also open up markets for Indian goods in Eastern Europe.

## Russia and Europe

The Russian soul, if it could be examined closely, would in all probability be composed of a European half and an Asian half. Over the centuries there have been various pulls and pressures from both halves. After the advent of Peter the Great, the European half predominated for a long time. In the new century, the pulls and pressures could become even more exaggerated. According to Georgy Lukacs, "Emergent capitalism appeared as an important factor in the formation of European nations. After profound revolutionary struggles, it transformed the chaos of small medieval feudal governments into great nations in the most capitalistically developed part of Europe".[9] Individual countries of Europe—those who had the means that is—expanded across the world in the eighteenth, nineteenth and twentieth centuries. The second half of the twentieth century saw the retraction of the European powers by stages. Therefore, the retraction of Russia from Asia nearly forty years after the European colonial powers felt it prudent to pull out—some were forced out—follows a pattern, except that Russia happens geographically to embrace both continents. The stakes for Russia in Asia remain enormous as an existential imperative.

Surprisingly—perhaps not so surprisingly—while the importance of Asia could continue to grow it would be wrong to presume therefrom that Asian growth *ipso facto* denotes a downsizing of European importance. It would have been the case had the Cold War continued. The demise of the Soviet Union confers upon Europe a whole range of exciting options provided the Old Continent breaks away from the deeply ingrained habit of looking at the world from an American perspective, as a US appendage. It need no longer be the case.

It is time for Europe to get out of the shadow of America. It was America's pushing of its own agenda for world dominance that has prevented Europe from having a European world view for the twenty first century. A historical turning point has now been reached. Several new vistas open up on Europe's geopolitical horizon at the end of the Cold War. Most military experts concede that Europe does not face any real military threat in the foreseeable future. While this does not mean that Europe should lower its military guard it does mean that Europe should feel free to have an independent strategic vision based on what is good for Europe and the European neighbourhood, which is basically Asia and Africa. NATO, after all, came into being because of the Soviet menace. Russia by itself cannot possibly regain the same geographic, demographic or military mass.

Russia has to be co-opted into the European strategic vision. Going a step further, its leaders should envision a Europe stretching from Calais to Vladivostok. Europe would then stretch not from the Atlantic to the Urals, but in a grand sweep from Atlantic to the Pacific. Examined dispassionately, freed from the Cold War mindset, the proposal envisages a pivotal role for the extended European Union as one of the most significant pillars of the global equipoise of the new millennium. Any number of difficulties can be conjured up by skeptics and naysayers. European statesmen should seize the initiative to usher in a new era. Russian leadership can hardly be averse to the idea once it sinks in. The Russian people would be enthusiastic about it. As possibly would be the average European citizen.

At some stage the Russian nuclear arsenal could be integrated into a common European defence as a measure of global stability. Thereafter, the process of nuclear disarmament would gather momentum. The P5 negotiating entities could, through a process of give and take, become just three major negotiating entities, namely, USA, the enlarged European Union and China. In anticipation of the possible turn of events in the direction indicated, Russia and Europe should join hands to prevent another Cold War from descending on the world. The more menacing cold war that is sought to be imposed unilaterally by the USA on a world that has barely begun to recover from the aftermath of the previous one. Europe occupies a unique position in the East-West dialogue. It should encourage Russia to resist acceding to American blandishments for diluting the 1972 ABM Treaty, a cornerstone of the global equipoise that nearly came into being before the US started once again flexing its military muscle. Should Europe decide to resolutely oppose the American NMD and TMD deployments—as it is instinctively inclined to do—the US would hardly be in a position to initiate a new arms race, one more terrifying in some ways than the earlier one after World War II. Europe must remember that should a free-for-all take place on account of the nuclear and missile proliferation that would surely follow a NMD deployment decision the battleground for any conflagration would be the Eurasian landmass. America is smug and secure beyond the oceans. Europe's vulnerability was during the Cold War—and will remain in any future war—an order of magnitude higher than that of USA. The Americans are aware of it. So, for that matter, are the Europeans; and yet the 'conditioned' inertia.

To quote from the 'Foreign Policy Concept of the Russian Federation' which was approved by the President, Mr. Putin on June 28, 2000:

"The Russian Federation views the EU as one of its main political and economic partners and will strive to develop with it an intensive, stable and long-term co-operation devoid of expediency fluctuations".

## Russia and USA

Russia was down—and almost out—at the end of the Cold War. The US obviously wanted at that stage to give a *coup de grâce* to the rump Russia not satisfied even after the break up of the Soviet Union. Had it sat back to consider its future course of action with wisdom and maturity it would have realised that the course that it adopted for dealing with Russia was not the one to take. Once again the American military-industrial complex forced the issue. Many in Europe voiced their misgivings. As had been its wont in the past the US brushed aside all objections—which in any case were put forward only tentatively, such being the status of the once proud Europeans now herded into collective submission.

The quote that follows is from the Russell-Einstein Manifesto, the credo of Pugwash that was issued in July 1955 and was signed by eleven distinguished scientists, most of them Nobel Prize winners. They drew attention to mankind's predicament in language that was, in a way, prophetic:

"We are speaking on this occasion, not as members of this or that nation, continent, or creed, but as human beings, members of the species man, whose continued existence is in doubt..." and called upon scientists to: *"remember your humanity and forget the rest"*

The US government failed to respond to this sane piece of advice and went on instead to usher in a global arms race that brought the planet to the brink of disaster more than once in one of the most tense periods of world history. It ended with the end of the Cold War, or so it seemed at that time. Now, after fifty years, the American government seems bent upon starting another arms spiral, far more menacing than the earlier one, by its insistence on going ahead unilaterally with the deployment of National Missile Defence.

Zbigniew, Brzezinski, National Security Adviser to President Carter, in an article, has remarked: "The US has never followed a genuinely universal and non-discriminatory policy of halting proliferation. In fact, US policy all along has been that of selective and preferential proliferation..."

## Concluding Remarks

In the 43rd session of the UN General Assembly, a typical year, the US voted against all of the 25 resolutions to enhance international security and for disarmament. The Western democracies in general and the US establishment in particular have yet not grasped the real import of the altered global reality. That the USA and Russia need no longer look at each other as adversaries but as partners in bringing about an end to all types of threats hanging over the viability of the Planet. What is being witnessed is the latent effect of the Cold War era continuing to manifest itself in the military-industrial complex of the former adversaries. As things stand now, and projecting the same template well into the future, it is difficult to see as to how Russia can again match the might of the United States. Russia can become a strong medium to high ranking power, but not a superpower in the 21$^{st}$ century. China could, at some stage reach fairly close to the superpower status. It will still not be able to match the might of the United States if one goes by the criterion of a superpower described at the beginning of the presentation. The only grouping that could surpass—not challenge—the United States by the same criteria would be a European Union stretching from the Atlantic to Vladivostok. Such an entity if it does come about could be the harbinger of the equipoise of the third millennium. (End of Presentation)

## The Prospect Ahead

The results of the December 7 (2003) election in Russia showed that the people of Russia appreciate the firm hand of Vladimir Putin at the helm of affairs. The near annihilation of pro-Western Liberal Parties at the hands of nationalists in the parliamentary elections strengthened the President. For the first time in Russia's post-Communist history, radical liberals were shut out of Parliament. The Union of Rightist Forces (SPS), led by the architects of the Yeltsin reform, Yegor Gaidar and Anatoly Chubais, got less than four percent of the vote, short of the five percent minimum needed to win seats in the State Duma, the Lower House of the Russian Parliament. The wave of public disillusionment with the results of the reforms also buried the other main liberal party, Yabloko.

Observers in Russia felt that Putin's campaign to dismantle oligarchic capitalism had an important security dimension which the Kremlin played down for political reasons. The arrest of Mikhail Khodorkovsky disrupted a multi-billion dollar deal for the purchase for Exxon Mobil of up to 40 percent in Yukos, which at that time was finalizing a merger with another Russian oil major, Sibneft. Exxon Mobil was believed to have bought up earlier more than 13 percent of Yukos' shares traded on the stock market. Had the deal come through, Exxon Mobil and British Petroleum, which had earlier acquired a controlling share in the Russian oil company, TNK, would have controlled 150 to 160 million tonnes of Russian oil production, or one-third of the country's annual output. Many in Russia felt that had this deal gone through it would have amounted to a dilution of Russian sovereignty.

The election results augur well for President Putin. He seems assured of an easy reelection. It is also likely that forces loyal to the Kremlin would command a two-thirds majority in the next Duma. It would mean that Putin would then be able to bring in changes to the Constitution. Experts suggested that he may seek to change the rule to limit the President to two terms in office. Most importantly, however, President Putin could use his vast new authority to change Russia by rebuilding its economy and national power. Avoiding ideological extremes he could use the state as the engine of change.

## Coming in from the Past

*Sri Aurobindo on Russia** : the piece was written just when the Russian Revolution had taken place in 1918-19.

"The outstanding portent of things to come is the continued existence, success, unbroken progress of the

---

*. [SABCL] *The Human Cycle,* vol.15 p. 642.

Russian revolution. This event promises to be as significant in human history as the great overturn of established ideas and institutions initiated in France in the eighteenth century, and to posterity it may well be this and not the downfall of Germany for which the great war will be ever memorable. Its importance is quite independent of the merits and demerits or the chances of survival of the present Bolshevik regime. The Bolshevik dictatorship is admittedly only an instrument of transition, a temporary concentration of revolutionary force, just as the Supreme Council and all that it supports is a temporary concentration of the opposing conservative forces. The achievements of this extraordinary government have been of a sufficiently astonishing character. Assailed continually from within and without, ruthlessly blockaded and starved and deprived of all means of sustenance and action except those it could create for itself out of itself or else conquer, repeatedly brought to the verge of downfall, it has survived all difficulties and dangers and rather derived always new strength from misfortune, overcome its internal and withstood its external enemies, spread itself in Asia beyond its own borders, organised out of chaos a strong civil and military instrument, and has had the force in the midst of scarcity, civil strife and foreign menace to lay the initial basis of a new type of society. This miracle of human energy is in itself no more than that, a repetition under more unfavourable circumstances of the extraordinary achievement of the Jacobins during the French Revolution. More important is the power of the idea that is behind these successes and has made them possible. It is a fact of only outward significance that the Bolsheviks not so long ago threatened with the loss of Moscow are now on the road to Warsaw. It is of much more significance that the western Powers find themselves driven at last to negotiate with the first successful communist government of modern times still denounced by them as a monstrosity to be destroyed and a danger to civilisation. But the thing of real significance is not these events that might have gone and might still go otherwise and might turn out to be only an episode; it is rather this fundamental fact affecting future possibilities that *a great nation marked out as one of the coming leaders of humanity* has taken a bold leap into the hidden gulfs of the future, abolished the past foundations, made and persisted in a radical experiment of communism, replaced middle-class parliamentarism by a new form of government and used its first energy of free life to initiate an entirely novel social order. It is acts of faith and audacities of this scale that change or hasten the course of human progress. It does not follow necessarily that what is being attempted now is the desirable or the definite form of the future society, but it is a certain sign that a phase of civilisation is beginning to pass and the Time-Spirit preparing a new phase and a new order."

## End Notes

1. Published in *United Service Institution of India Journal*, vol. CXXXI, no. 543, January-March 2001.
2. Yevgeny Kozhokin, *The Times of India*, 4 October 2000.
3. 'Where Ho, Mr. Putin' by Valentina Fedorova, *The Statesman*, 25 September 2000.
4. Georgy Lukacs, *Lenin: A Study on the Unity of his Thoughts.*
5. Andrei Bely, *Petersburg,* Penguin Books, p.65. Writing about Petersburg Vladimir Nabokov had this to say 'My greatest masterpieces of twentieth-century prose are in this order: Joyce's Ulysses; Kafka's Metamorphosis; Bely's Petersburg; and the first half of Proust's fairy tale, Remembrance of Things Past'. *The New York Times Book Review* called it 'The most important, most influential and most perfectly realized Russian novel written in the twentieth century'.
6. RK Dasgupta in *The Statesman* referring to A Aronson, 'Europe Looks at India', 1946.
7. *Asiaweek,* 22 September 2000.
8. *Middle East International,* no.629, 10 March 2000.
9. Georgy Lukacs, n. 4.

# 6

## *The Futility of National Missile Defences[1]

"It's a paper tiger—fierce enough to frighten away cowards only"-Sha Zukang, China's top disarmament official, on the potential threat of the proposed U.S. Missile-Defence System.[2]

Russia has already gone on record to the effect that it had enough weapons to counter any anti-ballistic missile system, and has threatened to deploy more atomic warheads if Washington builds a National Missile Defence System. This was reported in the *Washington Post* on 26 October 1999. The *Post* quoted Nikolai Mikhailov, first deputy defence minister, as saying a day earlier that Russia's arsenal has such "technical capabilities" to overcome any anti-missile defences. He said that the technology was available and would be used if the USA pushes us towards it.

---

* Based on talk delivered by the author at the United Service Institution of India, New Delhi on 8 March 2000. The article was circulated in the MIT by Noam Chomsky and the USFSS (US Federation of Scientists and Scholars) by the convenor.

The genesis of the paper on the futility or, more aptly, utility of national missile defence (NMD) goes back to the closing decades of the last century, to the launching of the Strategic Defence Initiative by the Reagan administration in the USA. Nearly twenty years down the road from the time that the initiative first impinged on the global consciousness the world is witnessing the birth of a deadlier, more menacing arms race on a planet already reeling under the wounds inflicted by the twentieth century. This paper endeavours to challenge the basic premise on which rests the unilateral step that the USA appears well on the way to taking.

It should be possible to commence with the assertion that not only will NMD/TMD not provide the desired immunity to USA but that it could end up by actually imperiling the security of its principal allies, Canada, Europe and Japan.

## Examining the Proposal

The national missile defence being considered by the USA can be examined from several differing perspectives: European, Russian, Chinese, Japanese, Canadian, Indian to name a few, as also the overall global perspective. These countries will have to factor in the new development into their own defence planning in the years ahead. How each entity would be affected would become apparent further on. Looking first at the motivation of the proponents of NMD in the USA, one can straightaway discern the streams in their thinking that must have led the military-industrial complex to push for a system that could severely jolt the existing global equilibrium, which by any reckoning, is heavily tilted in 'favour' of the United States of America.

The defence planners in USA would have calculated that should they be able to get away with NMD—which is tantamount to having one's cake and eating it too—they would derive two distinct advantages from the potentially hazardous venture. By their reckoning, these advantages boil down to:

- Affording themselves sufficient immunity against retaliation through NMD deployment. They could safely proceed, thereafter, to use mini nukes, a few years down the line, to neutralise the potential of their lesser adversaries, the so-called 'rogue' states. The other major powers would hardly be in a position to do anything about it except voice protests—as was the case with the bombing of Yugoslavia, where the relative impotence of Russia and China was clearly demonstrated. Of course, the USA would retain the option to add to, or subtract from, the list of rogue states at will.
- The second big advantage would accrue through the imperceptible strengthening of NMD to give them a qualitative edge over their major potential adversaries, currently Russia and China. (The anxiety over the rogue states hitting continental USA could merely be a smokescreen).

Arguments like these would, no doubt, have been used to persuade the U.S. government to seek the abrogation of a treaty that not only held for nearly three decades, but one which was well on the way to becoming the bedrock for other treaties of a similar nature; treaties that should have laid the groundwork for the emerging global equilibrium of the new millennium. There would certainly have been doubts in some quarters on the efficacy of NMD in a 'fog of war' scenario, as opposed to the near perfect launch conditions when carrying out proving tests. Notwithstanding such doubts, the Pentagon experts (much emboldened by their bombing successes of the nineties decade) in their presentations to the concerned committees would hardly be taking into account the fact that the lessons derived from the Gulf War and the bombing of Yugoslavia were not entirely correct. In the first case, they had overwhelming superiority; and, more importantly, there was no disruption of the decision-making process: of the chains of command in continental USA, intermediate command posts in Europe, Turkey and the Middle East. It was a clean run all the way to the target countries. Very perfect operating conditions indeed.

The recent failure of its anti-ballistic missile system to hit a speeding warhead high over the Pacific Ocean should have its lessons for the U.S. Defence Department. This was a clear indication that where highly advanced electronic technology is involved, requiring checks for ensuring hundred percent flawless performances of all the inputs prior to every launch, there would be no question of success turning out to be repeatable. This becomes clear from the Pentagon's disclosure that there had been technical problems associated with the test, which had become more difficult because of its having to be integrated with the ground-based radar in Hawaii and Kwajalein. If, as it appears, successive launchings of the missile system require such integration with a global radar network, it further compounds the uncertainties of missile launches.

The elaboration became necessary to show that perfect co-ordination at several levels and at several points becomes necessary to achieve a perfect intercept. It also shows that the adversary contemplating a strike could take collateral measures to degrade the intercept mechanism at any or several intermediate link points. In the previous (successful) test a modified unarmed Minuteman ICBM fired from California was intercepted and destroyed over the Pacific Ocean by a "kill vehicle" fired from the Marshall Islands. The kill device developed by Raytheon Co. carried aloft by a rocket, was (reportedly) a machine shaped somewhat like a television camera that weighed 55 kg and was 55 inches long. *It carries a computer that enables it to determine its location by the position of certain stars and then selects the target and attacks.* The test, worth 100 million dollars was the first of about 20 NMD system trials planned for the next six years.

Here, one needs to keep in mind the 'fudging' indulged in by almost all R&D agencies in the world, India not excluded. In unholy alliance with their prime contractors every subterfuge is applied to extract the next tranche of funds. Positive outcomes are played up. Negative outcomes underplayed. Conscientious scientists and potential whistle-blowers are kept at arm's length. To anyone seriously examining the NMD proposal from a technical viewpoint it becomes reasonably clear that the chances of such deployment actually meeting its stated aims—which are more for public consumption—would be remote. Should that be the case, realisation begins to dawn, with mounting horror, that the real aim of the proponents of NMD—and here we go to the heart of the military-industrial complex—is to promote another arms race knowing full well that they are miles ahead of the rest of the world (or so they believe) due to the SDI of the Reagan era and the tens of billions of dollars already spent on it. They want to recover that amount by forcing the world to move in that direction while they themselves change direction after deployment of NMD. Their scientists already 'have' some tentative counters to TMD in case the rest of the world catches up. The rest of the world's nations, not at all interested in another global arms race, must do something 'now' while they can. The *post facto* stage, once deployment is effected, is not far off. Activities relating to NMD deployment are moving at a pace that can be termed as 'fast and furious'.

## Global Consequences of Deployment of NMD/TMD

Since, it is becoming fairly obvious that certain interests are hell-bent upon deploying NMD, regardless of the global consequences, it would be worth examining what those consequences could turn out to be. First and foremost, it will once again force colossal spending on defence research rather than on other planetary benefits. The psychological transition point of the new millennium for peace and goodwill on earth would lie shattered in the very first years of the new millennium.

The BMD system merits attention for the technology headway, which the U.S. has made for ensuring that it stays ahead with the massive destructive capabilities it has built up for the wars it might wage in the future. The response to any such move on the part of the U.S. from countries that do not feel comforted by the trend would be to fortify themselves adequately. There are indications that Russia is already very much disturbed by the U.S. Washington should, therefore, keep in mind the response that an offensive military strategy could provoke.

The U.S. action—intentionally, or otherwise—could provoke elements inimical to U.S. hegemony to step up their activities, thereby making the Americans more paranoid about their own security. A few examples will suffice:

- The USA is creating another 44 Rapid Assessment and Initial Detection (RAID) teams to add to the 10 created earlier, and designed to counter chemical or biological weapon (CBW) attacks by terrorists.
- The U.S. Department of Defence is considering relocation of the offices of senior civilian and military officials in the vast Pentagon complex due to what is perceived as their increased vulnerability to sniper fire, rocket-propelled grenades and other potential terrorist threats, according to officials.

All this would lead the U.S. military into another mad spiral of counter, then counter counter, followed by counter counter counter as was seen in the electronic counter measures spiral of the earlier decades. It would be recalled that ECM was followed, soon thereafter, by ECCM and so on. Before the ordinary folk in the United States become any the wiser they would be ensconced in the last 'gilded ghetto' on the planet, their sky and shorelines would bristle with sensors, sprint missiles, SWAT, RAID and other quick reaction, counter measure teams. Almost everyone 'out there' would become a potential Red (or the modern day derivative of the proverbial enemy of the Cold War). *

The active supporters of NMD do not realise that although the other countries have held themselves back so far by honouring the spirit of the 1972 ABM Treaty, it should not be imagined that they have not been anxiously watching the developments in the USA. At 1/10$^{th}$ or possibly 1/100$^{th}$ or maybe even 1/1000$^{th}$ the cost of the US programme, NMD, in all probability, will be effectively neutralised in less than three to five years, if not earlier, thus resulting in the pouring down the drain of a few hundred billion dollars of the US taxpayers money and a much greater toll of the environment of the planet. No sane person should be contemplating such fiendish horrors for the living organisms on the planet.

At this juncture it should be possible to briefly tabulate the reactions that could take place in the countries that would immediately be affected, in some form or the other, by outright abrogation or violation of the 1972 ABM Treaty.

* The talk was delivered by the author in New Delhi and USA (Orlando) full eighteen months prior to 9/11/2001.

- Chinese reportedly monitoring U.S. forces through 17 spy satellites. Other countries could be obliged to follow suit.
- NMD, in actual fact, ratifies and perpetuates for another century the subordinate status of Japan, Canada and continental Europe after the demise of the Cold War.
- It would lead to the deployment and proliferation of sub strategic nuclear weapons on surface vessels and attack submarines. The attack submarines would not have to be the sophisticated type. Rather, the philosophy of deployment would shift to the low grade, low-cost Soviet and Chinese tactic of employment of mass—*low cost saturation of phenomenally high cost systems.*
- At the present time Russia does not have sufficient power to prevent the West from taking advantage of its weakness. The U.S. action might force the Russians to boldly change tack.
- Russia, as a consequence of the U.S. actions, is reportedly offering China the use of its space-based navigation system (GLONASS) for a joint counter to the U.S. NMD initiative.
- China would become even more non-amenable to fissile materials cut-off.
- North Korea would virtually be goaded into stepping up missile production. So would many other nations.
- In as far as it relates to France it would be worth recalling President Francois Mitterand's famous 1983 statement. He said, "le dissuasion, c'est moi". He elaborated that the decision to use nuclear weapons belongs to the President of the French Republic and

to him only. In classical French nuclear thinking, there can be no form of decision-sharing, since the 'autonomy of decision' is the guarantee of national independence and of French strategic sovereignty. The possibility of the French reverting to the neo-Gaullist independent military posture cannot be ruled out.

- U.S. and Japanese officials are expected to shortly finalise, if they haven't already done so, a joint theatre missile defence research programme. They are also considering positioning the radar from a developmental theater high-altitude area defence (THAAD) system in Japan. The Chinese could well respond by setting up a perimeter along the Spratly Islands all the way to North Korea, resulting in the total destruction of the marine ecosystem in areas that are perilously fragile. (Apparently, few people seem to care).
- TMD will force the development and deployment of tactical nuclear weapons so that the adversary can have the satisfaction of at least some damage of sufficient intensity to U.S. forces deployed in other theatres, 'outside' continental USA: making all such elements sacrificial goats. Unless, that is, the Pentagon is planning to saturate the globe with NMD, dozens of local TMD and the mobile navy theatre wide (NTW) shipboard missile defence systems. Once violated, violating other clauses of the ABM Treaty would scarcely matter.
- India will no doubt be obliged to take into account the new military escalation being forced upon war-weary humanity.
- There has to be a ripple effect extending to Iran and so many other countries. And so the spiral goes on and on and on.

The tragedy is that sane voices will get drowned out when the military dimension once again pushes all other dimensions of human endeavour into the background. It has happened before, and after the First and Second World Wars. Even as the CTBT debate is raging, research on fourth generation nuclear weapons is proceeding apace in the U.S. and other countries, mainly the P5. A possibility being considered is the use of a non-fission trigger for fusion devices. The Nobel laureate Hans Bethe in a letter to President Clinton in April 1997 emphasised that the U.S. should cease work on all the new types of nuclear weapons, including the pure fusion devices. Similar appeals by some of the most eminent scientists of the twentieth century went unheeded.

It should be obvious to anyone looking at the NMD initiative that the military-industrial complex is further strengthening—or so it thinks—the defences of continental U.S.A. at the cost of their allies of the last century, namely, Canada, Western Europe, Japan, South Korea and many lesser allies. They are providing strategic depth to continental U.S.A. and nothing else. It hardly needs reiteration that for the foreseeable future, and even beyond, nobody would be thinking of attacking Western Europe or Canada in the military sense. After NMD/TMD becomes a reality they automatically become the battleground for the next major war. Their second-class status will get congealed for the twenty first century. What Canada and West Europe provide for the defence of continental USA from the east and north gets replicated from the other direction by Japan, Taiwan and South Korea. It would not entirely displease the military-industrial complex in the new century were China, Japan, North Korea or South Korea to lock horns in any regional internecine combination and dissipate their military and economic strengths. This would be the most likely outcome once TMD is set up over the Pacific Ocean marine littoral of Asia. All these countries must enter into a regional dialogue to secure their future.

Statesmen, scientists and intellectuals must shed their Cold War mindsets and consciously sit back to take stock of where they are headed. They must analyse whether the direction being taken is a conscious, well-reasoned decision for the common good or whether having stultified into the Cold War mental gridlock they are being propelled into another dangerous drift against their better judgment. Such an analysis on the part of West European nations becomes essential for not only the good of Europe but for the good of the world as a whole. Canada and Europe are about the only entities at this point in time who could take a firm stand against the new U.S. global deployments. They must act now, while it is possible to definitively check the deadly descent toward another global conflagration—not immediately perhaps, but in the not too distant future.

Why only Europeans or Canadians? Should concerned people in the U.S., not directly involved with the pork barrel politics surrounding the military industrial complex, decide to examine the NMD/TMD proposal dispassionately, they too would discover the unreality of the proposal. Dozens of low-cost options would be available for neutralising the efficacy of the new deployment being contemplated. NMD can demonstrate its efficacy in carefully orchestrated tests under ideal conditions, but would not be in a position to do so under imperfect warlike conditions. For, an adversary wanting to beat the NMD would surely take collateral measures that could lead to a premature release of retaliatory nuclear might, resulting in a global holocaust.

## Several Pathways for Neutralisation of NMD

In this paper an attempt is being made to list out, in a very rudimentary fashion, the diverse pathways that would be available to neutralise NMD. Any or several pathways could be developed, not only by the so-called rogue states, but by military-industrial groups of many countries, for the sake of developing the counter to a new military menace on the global horizon, simply because it exists. To name just a few:

- Suicide missions with mini-nuclear weapons.
- Next stage would be robots doing the same things.
- Ships with land attack missile systems. Once these proliferate the coastguard would not know whether the innocent-looking trawler lying off just beyond the exclusive maritime zone posed a real threat or not. (Ergo, another fifty or hundred special teams to counter a potential menace of this nature on the west as well as the east coast. In which case special forces would have to be kept as standby for the Panama Canal Zone; not knowing whether the Hong Kong-based Chinese company operating the canal had been infiltrated by the triads, or other elements inimical to U.S interests.
- New shielding materials which considerably reduce the capability of several types of sensors and ordinary detection monitors. Hence, there would be proposals for another billion dollars to deploy more sophisticated instruments overhead, at every available point, night and day. (This could soon become the new reality. It is not an exercise in *reductio ad absurdum*).
- Intermediate point mini nuclear bursts by decoy systems concomitant with the launch of main nukes. The fallout from decoys, countering systems etc. will

generally be over the oceans, Canada, Western Europe, Mexico, Japan, Taiwan and several other points, 'well away' from continental U.S.A. (The allies, expendable commodities *in extremis*, were always the first tier of U.S. defences).

- Decoy dirigibles.
- Physical destruction, laser blinding and electronic warfare are all likely to be employed to deny the enemy the use of his satellites. (Hence, false alarms, ruses to test U.S. systems and increased spying will lead to greater brinkmanship than in the Cold War era).
- Satellite neutralisation actions, concurrent with nuclear attack options, or independently. In the latter case, one could never be certain whether the destruction or loss of orbit was due to technical failure, inadvertence or mischief. If the latter, then mischief on whose part? After all, now there are many actors on the world stage who, in the twenty-first century, have the technical capability to interfere with another nation's or even a rival's commercial satellite. Such technologies are proliferating exponentially. (Meanwhile, systems can be swamped, driven out of their minds so to say, by being made to chase illusions, all the time, in a virtual reality world).
- Countering sensors at each stage i.e. the IR sensors on geo-synchronous orbits to detect the tremendous heat from a ballistic missile launch, seconds after launch. Possibility of testing out several different ways to simulate the launch activity and so on, at every stage.

- Weather modifications would become the next arena of the global destruction sweepstakes to neutralise certain types of sensors being utilised by TMD/NMD systems.
- Race for anti-satellite weapons will commence in real earnest.
- Ground-based ballistic missile defences, sea-based ballistic missile defences and other defences of this type will proliferate to newer regions of the world.
- Reverse simulation for defeating any system.
- False echoes at launch, mid-flight, terminal end. Gyrations etc.
- Computer hacking to start NMD/TMD launches. Disgruntled elements breaking the codes.
- Sub-critical flooding of the flight pathway.
- USAF mini-decoys may lead enemy missiles astray.
- MALD (miniature air-launched decoys).
- The U.S. Navy is eyeing UCAV (uninhabited combat air vehicle).

All these concepts, in their less sophisticated forms, are capable of being replicated by several adversaries, leading to further pollution for marine life and greater threat to continental U.S.A. in a world turned hostile.

## Ecological Consequences

At this stage it becomes necessary to pause a while to take note of the ecological consequences of the renewed military activity. Here is a report that is a grim reminder of what is in store:

> "Through explosive reactions, fires and the burning of great amounts of different materials and chemicals and through intensive actions of military airplanes, the millions of tons of oxygen that the living world needs, have been irretrievably spent."[3]

Very obviously, in spite of the alarm bells ringing from every corner of the globe on the dangerous levels of eco-destruction taking place, the military-industrial complex of the major power shows scant regard for such concerns.*

The increasing reliance on electronics in the so-called RMA is slowly destroying the life support sensory abilities of the myriad life forms inhabiting the planet. The world seems to have become oblivious to the needs of the other species. Soon enough it would become clear to every human being that today: "the dangers that we face from eco-destruction dwarf the mere problems of national security".

## Recommendations

Immediate action, therefore, needs to be taken at the global level by national governments, international organisations, nongovernmental organisations and the media to prevent the world from entering another arms race. Towards this end, recommendations that could conceivably ward off the looming catastrophe are tabulated below:

- Convening an emergency session of the UN General Assembly for calling a halt to the militarisation of space.
- UN Secretary General in concert with UNESCO, WHO, and other global organisations to issue a call for an immediate halt to NMD/TMD.
- UN Secretary General to nominate a panel of eminent global citizens to analyse the consequences of the militarisation of space.

---

* Reality seems to have finally intruded. A secret report warns of "rioting and nuclear war, Britain will be Siberian in 20 years, threat to the world is greater than terrorism".

*The Observer*, New York: 22 February 2004. Mark Townsend and Paul Harris, Pentagon tells Bush, 'Climate Change will Destroy Us'.

- Nation states opposed to the violation of the 1972 ABM Treaty in concert with Russia to approach the International Court of Justice.
- The world must guard against undue (and irresistible) pressure being put on Russia to accept dilution of the provisions of the 1972 ABM Treaty. (It is feared that attempts to buy Russian silence may well be under way. Note must be taken here of the rescheduling of the Russian debt. It is to be hoped that strings of this nature were not attached).
- The no-first-use (NFU) declaration by any state to have credibility would have to be 'unconditional and irrevocable' to really constitute a safeguard for the interim stage towards the abolition of nuclear weapons.
- The principle of 'supreme planetary interest' has to be the linchpin of future human progress and existence on earth. The military dimension is submerging the other dimensions that sustain life on the planet and enrich the cultural identity of nations and societies. SDI-related research could ultimately give yields that could turn out to be *trillion times* more powerful than current yields. Continuous pressure by nongovernmental organisations for the dismantlement of star war-type technologies.
- Global initiative for strengthening the 1972 ABM Treaty—to be converted into a binding global protocol.
- One of the respected U.S. philanthropic foundations could be persuaded to set up an independent 'environmental effects panel' to assess the damage to life forms once the NMD race kicks off and the current level of U.S. military activity related to NMD is multiplied by a factor of 10, 50 or even 100 as other nations start limbering up for the new 'planet

destruction sweepstakes'. The panelists could be from the U.S.A itself—respected intellectuals, scientists and environmentalists from outside the 'milscience' fraternity.

- An international, linux-type project on the internet for the citizens of the world to design add-on neutralisation modules to counter the P5 and force them into the dismantlement of NMD and subsequently nuclear weapons.
- Without prejudice to their existing military agreements China, Japan, North Korea, South Korea and Taiwan to nominate a panel of respected intellectuals, scientists and eminent citizens (not in the government) to study the likely environmental impact of enhanced military deployments in the region.
- A subsidiary panel to study alternative models of regional security for the twenty-first century. (Once such impartial studies are completed it would become eminently clear that the *only real security threat to the region is from retaining the security models of the twentieth century.* All these run counter to the actual aspirations of the peoples of these countries).
- Russia, China and Japan to become joint signatories for guaranteeing the territorial integrity of South Korea. Phased withdrawal of U.S. military presence in South Korea by 2010.
- China to pledge to maintain sufficient pressure on North Korea for eschewing militarism. The regional co-sponsors (China, Russia and Japan) to jointly work for the peaceful reunification of Korea.
- China to deposit an affidavit (pledge) before the International Court of Justice that it would never use force for the reunification of Taiwan.

- Taiwan would pledge to respect the principle of reunification, in three stages: stage 1—free commerce and exchange between it and the mainland of China up to 2025; stage 2—Taiwan accepts integration, but would retain full provincial autonomy under an 'irrevocable' Article 370 type dispensation (as in the case of the Indian province of Jammu & Kashmir).
- Phased dismantling of the Japan-USA security pact(s) by 2020.
- China, Japan, South Korea (eventually reunified Korea), Vietnam, Philippines and Taiwan to enter a peace and tranquility pact for the maintenance of peace in the maritime littoral of the Asia-Pacific region and for the eco-revival of the region.
- The Spratly Islands to be managed by a joint holding company for sustainable exploitation of resources. An independent tribunal to be established for working out the pro rata holding pattern between the claimants. The award to be ratified by all the concerned countries and the instrument to be deposited at the International Court of Justice. Full demilitarisation of Spratly Group of islands by 2005.
- U.S. senate to invite a committee of national and international experts to independently verify the claims of the U.S. Departments of Defence and State on the efficacy of the NMD proposal as well as its likely global ramifications.
- Global regulatory military satellite (milsat) body to prevent milsats from proliferating exponentially in lower and upper atmosphere regions and perhaps in outer space as well. This global body would be in the form of a joint holding company with shares allocated to state and non-state actors. A golden share would be held by the global regulatory body

that would be responsible for depositing the instruments and articles of association with the International Court of Justice and the International Criminal Court. It would automatically make 'milsat' data available to all state and non-state parties on a purely commercial basis, thus obviating the need for national military satellites. If nations don't agree, a group of world citizens to go ahead. Transparency paramount.

- Need for an international approach on issues that threaten mankind as a whole.
- Five-year moratorium to be agreed to, in principle, for the prevention of all military space activities. This period would become the interregnum for the drafting of global protocols for the demilitarisation of the planet in a phased manner.

## Concluding Remarks

"The United States of America has become the undisputed leader in the field of scientific growth. Never before in the history of mankind has any one nation dominated the world in so many diverse ways. U.S.A. is truly the hub of the world whichever way the wheel of mankind's destiny spins in the coming millennium. Even if it stops spinning America is the only country, which has the technological potential to restart the spin. Tragically it is also at the forefront of the race that could write 'finis' to the tale of mankind". [4]

Today, and for the foreseecable future, the fate of mankind is in the hands of U.S.A. The rest of the world can keep making noises at the periphery. It will make scant difference. It is only when the U.S. establishment is persuaded to reverse direction, will the world change direction—in the right direction. The problem is now time-critical. We are in a situation where the super laboratories of the world are working overtime with large monetary grants to design more and more lethal forms of destructive mechanisms. Once these see the light of day they will again force increased spending on defence research into areas that can defeat NMD; with consequences not yet projected onto the global consciousness. By now it is well known that no political decision to govern the conduct of military operations can hope to work once initial control has been transferred to the military. Invariably, maximum overkill and saturation attacks would follow. The psychological transition point of the new millennium, the hoped for harbinger of peace and goodwill on earth, lies shattered in the first few years of the new era. This brings one to the most fundamental question of humankind's existence in the world today. The question reads:

"Why are the overwhelming majority of the citizens of the world, fully aware of the consequences to the planet of another arms race—potentially more virulent than that of an earlier era—walking away from their responsibility—to themselves, to successor generations and to all life forms on the planet"?

In 1945 at the conclusion of World War II the Cold War intervened, leaving the rest of the world with little choice. Another historical opportunity at global harmonisation is being missed at the turn of the millennium. As at the turn of the last century the global decision-makers are primarily the leaders of the Western world. This could turn out to be their last chance in world history to usher in a harmonious world order. Can they measure up to the challenge—and opportunity?

Irrationality is fast becoming the order of the day. The world is being conditioned to live with insanity. Palaeontologists tell us that extinctions of an order of magnitude have occurred on earth every 65 million years or so. These have generally been attributed to cosmic events. The last such extinction saw the disappearance of the dinosaurs. This time round the extinction is being programmed by the most evolved being—for himself and for those sentient beings that nurtured human existence on the planet for millions of years and provided companionship to this evolved creature.

Today the global mass is yearning for arms control, reduction of armaments and disarmament. The straining at the leash by the military-industrial complex represents a diametrically opposite urge—the rearmament of the planet and the militarisation of space. It runs counter to whatever humanity stands for at the present time. Should the 1972 ABM Treaty be abrogated, or violated, then, hypothetically at least, every convention, treaty and protocol would stand (potentially) abrogated; and the consensus built up painstakingly over half a century would be destroyed, leading to global anarchy on a scale which would have been difficult to comprehend in the century we have just left behind.

All systems are amorphous and constantly mutating. The ordinary people across the globe would never come to know as to what new types of monsters were being spawned in the spawning hatcheries being set up in different parts of the globe; top-secret laboratories pulsating with hideous planet-destroying creations. The aim of this presentation was to demonstrate the fallacy of the concept of immunity provided by NMD.

The dawn of the new millennium represents a window of opportunity for the world. After several decades, if not centuries, the great nations of the world who have the arsenals to destroy the world, have arrived at a momentary global equipoise where no insurmountable tension exists between any of the major powers. A remarkable interregnum, representing possibly the opportunity of the millennium. The peoples of the world should have been entering the new millennium with joy in their hearts and a song on their lips. The military-industrial complex deems it otherwise.

The presentation ends with a quote from one of the great Americans of the last century:

> "You cannot organize civilisation around the core of militarism and at the same time expect reason to control human destinies".
>
> -Franklin D Roosevelt.

## Update

In the coming years the US Missile Defence Agency (MDA) is planning to unveil its anti-missile defence system. Ten interceptors designed to destroy long-range ballistic missiles will be lowered into their silos in California and Alaska. These, it is felt, will destroy long-range ballistic missiles launched by 'rogue' regimes. In theory, the basis of the programme is that a threatening missile will be detected by satellites soon after its launch and its trajectory tracked by radar. Thereafter, an interceptor will be dispatched from California or Alaska. Out in space, the exo-atmospheric kill vehicle (EKV) will separate from its booster, and collide with the attacking missile at about 15,000 miles per hour. Initially, the interceptors—ten in 2004–2005 with another ten to follow – are intended to provide limited capability against attack by a second rank hostile power or an accidental launch. To begin with the system will be limited to countering threats emanating from northeast Asia. By 2005, the coverage could extend to the Middle East.

The system, based on shooting down a limited number of missiles during the mid-course phase of the trajectory is generally akin to the system first proposed by the Bill Clinton administration. The add-on elements, scheduled to become operational from 2005, are designed to destroy short-and medium-range missiles with interceptor fire from ships. Many of the technologies designed to tackle missiles in their boost phase have still not been perfected. Space-based weapons would be a long way off. Criticisms abound about the system being rudimentary or unreliable. Experts have felt that the trials carried out so far were 'tailored' to meet with success so that funding for subsequent phases could proceed. As far as the question of costs is concerned the MDA is likely to get around $9 billion a year for the next five years. Not many people are hazarding a guess as to the cost of operationalising the various systems on the MDA drawing board. One think tank reportedly mentioned a figure of $1 trillion.[5]

An array of arguments are likely to be marshaled by the proponents and opponents of the systems that the MDA is proposing to set up in the coming years, at heavy outlays. Going beyond the arguments advanced in Washington what can be said with near certainty is that an independent set of experts chosen from across the world are more than likely to question the efficacy of the system. Moreover, the levels of sophistication already reached by Russia and likely to be reached by several other countries, including China, Japan and India would easily penetrate the anti-missile shields being put up by the U.S.A.

North Korea has often been cited as the 'rogue state' for which such defences would prove useful. These are theoretical constructs advanced by lobbies attached to the armaments manufacturers linked to the programme. A large portion or at least a significant portion of their budgets are conceivably being spent in getting favourable comments from experts so that their funding is not jeopardized. When taking North Korea as a case study the proponents of the scheme forget that they are again tailoring the threat perception to advance their programme, actual efficacy being a secondary issue. Should the programme not prove efficacious after one or two decades, and after expending tens of billions of dollars, it can be shelved or put on the back-burner. Meanwhile, the current proponents of the far-fetched scheme would have moved on; they would no longer be accountable in their dotage or from the next world. In the North Korean case not one of them has offered to discuss the alternatives available to North Korea. For example, why should the North Korean regime target continental U.S.A, when it can just as easily inflict unacceptable damage to U.S. interests in Asia.

By the same reckoning, none of the states in the Middle East could conceivably be thinking of going in for programmes that involve hitting U.S.A. with intercontinental ballistic missiles. They have already found out that U.S.A. can be hit pretty hard, again and again, through a myriad ways that do not require such tremendous outlays. At the end of the day, when independent analysts sift through the chaff thrown up by the proponents of the systems being put in place under the aegis of the MDA, it becomes apparent that as in the case of so many other decisions taken by the U.S. administration recently, efficacy, accountability or logic has hardly anything to do with the decisions. Interests that are the mainstay of the establishment have to be given their due. Both the oil and the armament lobbies are the holy cows. They cannot be touched under the existing dispensation.[6]

## End Notes

1. Published in the *United Service Institution of India Journal*, Vol. CXXX, no.539, January-March 2000. Also circulated in the MIT by Noam Chomsky and USFSS (US Federation of Scientists and Scholars) by the convenor.

2. *Asiaweek*, 4 February 2000.
3. Report of the inter-agency needs assessment mission dispatched by the Secretary General of the United Nations to the Federal Republic of Yugoslavia.
4. Vinod Saighal *Third Millennium Equipoise*, New Delhi: Lancer Publishers, 1998 p x.
5. See also the *Economist*, 6 December 2003, pp. 29-30.
6. Vinod Saighal *Restructuring Pakistan*, New Delhi: Manas Publications, 2002 p, 182.

# 7

# * The Demographic Dynamic of the 21st Century

## Introduction

'We shall require a new manner of thinking, if mankind is to survive'.**

Simply put, the demographic dynamic entails essentially the resolution of the contradiction between two diametrically opposed projections: the demographic one of the world population reaching 10 to 12 billion by the year 2050; and the scientific estimate that the earth's long-term carrying capacity may not be much greater than a few billion. Because of this widening hiatus between what would be available and what the burgeoning population will need to live adequately, a sea change has to occur in the propagation and consumption patterns of human beings the world over.

What then would be an 'adequate' standard of living for the majority of human beings in the 21st century?

---

* Paper presented by the author at the UNESCO-sponsored Millennium Symposium on Science, Society & Human Rights, 24-26 August 2000 at Regina, Canada.

** Albert Einstein.

Obviously, there would be a need to moderate the lifestyles at the two extremes: between the hedonistic over-consumption taking place amongst the most affluent at one end and the almost sub-human existence experienced by the most wretched of the earth at the other. Rather than quantifying this mean by the modern yardstick of number of telephones, automobiles, per capita consumption of one item or the other, it would perhaps be more appropriate to settle for the view expressed by the French mathematician Marquis de Condorcet, who wrote in 1795:

"Population growth can be limited if people have a duty towards those who are not yet born; that duty is not to give them *existence* but to give them *happiness.*"

The scope of the subject being vast it is intended to examine it in two parts: beginning with the most pressing global aspects; followed by the ground reality as it exists in vast swathes of the over-populated countries in Asia and Africa, notably the subcontinent; groupings that contribute in a big way to population over-pressures on the planet. At the end of the paper—and following from the earlier examination—an attempt will be made to highlight areas that would require anticipatory global action by the global community acting in unison. At the very outset it needs to be stated that, by and large, demographic planners worldwide have come around to the view that women's education, emancipation and maternal and child health are the best means of achieving a manageable population growth. The problem in the near-term, however, is the widening gap in countries that need to do something about their burgeoning population and the resources available for implementing sensible poverty alleviation schemes. The problem is exacerbated by mismanagement on the part of people responsible for administering the schemes.

## Global Aspects

### The Demographic-Ecological Interface

The effects of the terrific population growth of the second half of the twentieth century have been so thoroughly documented that any further repetition becomes unnecessary. What should interest everybody is the price that the coming generations of not only humans, many other species as well, will have to pay for the wanton exploitation of natural resources. It stands to reason that one of the foremost global challenges resulting from rampant population growth relates to the demographic-ecological interface. Space and scarcities—land, air, water—have become the burning issues of the day. The first strategic threat to human societies and the flora and fauna (which gets largely ignored) comes from the global water scarcities that are being increasingly felt. Recuperation, restoration and redistribution of fresh water are becoming urgent concerns. The second important aspect related to water, in a different way perhaps, is global warming. The rise of sea-levels and the loss of low-lying coastal areas around the world could create migrations of populations on a scale seldom conceived of before in human history. Since one-third of humankind lives within 60 kilometers of the coastline, the number of refugees likely to be created will be unprecedented.

Although the sea-level has risen and fallen through different geological periods, never has the change been anywhere near as rapid as that now expected as a consequence of global warming. Nations like Bangladesh, India, Egypt, Gambia, Indonesia, Mozambique, Pakistan, Senegal, Surinam, Thailand and China, not to mention island nations like Maldives and Vanuatu (formerly New Hebrides), will be devastated if the projections now being made by scientists turn out to be accurate. Moreover, experts note that every coastal country will suffer adverse effects.

Here it would be pertinent to reproduce excerpts from AL Gore's book, *The Earth in Balance*:

- About ten million residents of Bangladesh will lose their homes and means of sustenance because of the rising sea-level, due to global warming, in the next few decades. Where will they go? Whom will they displace? What political conflicts will result? That is only one example. According to some predictions, not long after Bangladesh feels the impact, up to 60 percent of the present population of Florida may have to be relocated. Where will they go?
- Florida has already borne the brunt of one of the largest ecologically-induced migrations of this century. Some one million people emigrated from Haiti to the United States in the last decade—not only because of political oppression, but also because the worst deforestation and soil erosion in the world made subsistence farming impossible for them.
- Nearly one-third of humanity lives within 60 kilometers of a coastline. A rise in mean sea-level of only 25 centimeters would have substantial effects... a problem of an order of magnitude, which no one has ever had to face.... In virtually all countries the growing numbers of refugees would cast a dark and lengthening shadow.

Even the term 'sustainable development' though representing a well thought out strategy when first enunciated several decades ago has lost its meaning in many parts of the subcontinent—and the world at large. Sustainable development, among other attributes, referred largely to the tribal communities living in harmony with nature, exploiting the forest produce on a sustainable basis, giving room and time to nature to regenerate itself; no doubt, an excellent strategy. However, due to poor implementation on the ground, it lost its cutting edge in a few short decades. The premise on which it rested no longer holds good for many areas in the year 2000.

This requires elaboration. Taking the example of any given area where development was sought to be implemented on a sustainable basis, suppose that at the beginning there were *x* number of tribal people living off *y* square kilometers of forest area. After 50 years, what is the result on the ground? In most cases, the number of tribals—plus migrants who started encroaching on the same forest area—have become *x* multiplied by two, three or five; while the forest area, which was to have been exploited in a sustainable manner, has shrunk to half, one third, or at times even more than the original size.

From the foregoing it becomes apparent that here again unless the state intervenes decisively to restore the original forest area by removing encroachments and undertakes massive reforestation, concomitant with reversal of population growth, no planned development, sustainable, or any modification thereto, has any chance of success on the ground.

Although there is still a lot to learn about the symbiosis between forests and rain clouds, it *is* known that when the forests are destroyed, the rain eventually tapers off and brings less moisture. Ironically, the heavy rains continue to fall for a while where the forest used to be, washing away the top-soil that is no longer protected by the canopy of the trees or held in place by the root system.

It is estimated that should the exploitative trends in resource use continue and the world population grows as projected (8.9 billion by 2030, leveling off at 11.5 billion around 2150), then per capita availability of range land will drop by 22 percent and fish catch by 10 percent. The per capita area of irrigated land, which now yields about one-third of the global food harvest, will drop by 12 percent and cropland area and forest land per person will shrink by 21 percent and 31 per cent respectively. The world's economy by the middle of this century is expected to increase five times from the current level, causing depletion of the world's natural resources on a gigantic scale. Therefore, the crying need of the hour is to replace the existing growth models with newer models that will allow for the re-establishment of harmonious existence with nature—a pattern that had generally sustained humankind and animal-kind through the ages.

One tragic example of the loss of forests and then water is found in Ethiopia. The amount of its forested land has decreased from 40 to 1 percent in the last four decades. Concurrently, the amount of rainfall has declined to the point where the country is rapidly becoming a wasteland. The effects of the prolonged drought that has resulted have combined with the incompetence of its government to produce an epic tragedy: famine, civil war, and economic turmoil have wreaked havoc on an ancient and once-proud nation. (Al Gore, *The Earth in Balance*)

## Refugees: The Problem Magnified

The migration of people from one settlement to another or from one nation to another is as old as mankind itself. The history of the world is migration. A pattern that is not likely to change. The question in an era of growing numbers and shrinking resources is its management so that the rights of vulnerable communities are protected. Coming to the subcontinent of India the threat to India is not so much from Pakistani missiles and nuclear weapons in the new century. The threat to India will be demographic. India has to plan now for the economic threat that could materialise from a human influx that could result from the economic collapse of Pakistan.

The tolerance levels for refugees from war, want or persecution will be far less in the twenty-first century. Few advanced countries will accept them, as was the case in the second half of the twentieth century. Therefore, each region of the world will have to find its own methodologies for tackling the human—or possibly sub-human—surplus of the countries that comprise that region. India's northeast illustrates the point.

According to available figures the main reason for insurgency in the Indian state of Tripura has been the large influx of refugees and immigrants from East Pakistan (Bangladesh), which resulted in a dramatic change in the demography of the state. The tribal population, which was in a majority, became a minority. In 1947, the population of tribals in Tripura was 93 percent of the total population of 600,000, but by 1981 they had been reduced to a minority of 28.5 percent out of a population of 2.06 million.

In the absence of refugee-specific legislation, refugees tend to be governed by archaic laws meant to deal with foreigners and other aliens. As a result of this lack of understanding, refugees have often been summarily deported back to their country, endangering their life and liberty.

India had, in fact, maintained since long that the country's own traditions of tolerance and acceptance of refugees over the centuries has made adherence to any international protocol redundant. Its record of welcoming and sheltering refugees from the neighbourhood—be it Afghanistan, Bangladesh, Tibet, Sri-Lanka, to name four of the major refugee flows in the past 40 years—speaks for itself.

The refugee situation elsewhere may not be similar. To quote Jonathan Power: "Europe, a continent not used to immigration despite various waves throughout history, is not instinctively welcoming. Quite the reverse, its raw impulses are hostile. It is the working class who have to bear the social brunt of immigration, not the intellectuals or economists who explain its supposed benefits, even allure".[1]

Climate experts, writing about the trend in the Sahel and the mass famines and immigration that have accompanied it, feel that some national territories may, in the long run, become more or less uninhabitable if the trend persists. This would mean further large-scale migrations. Each year an additional 20 million hectares of agricultural land become too degraded for crop production or is lost to urban sprawl.

What is being referred to here is not demographic progression but *demographic distortion* on a scale with which neither human beings nor the planet can cope. The UN reported that as many as one million people fled incursions by Ethiopian troops deep into the southwestern region of Eritrea. Another 50,000 crossed into Sudan with thousands more expected to arrive.[2]

## Types of Migrations and their Long-Term Effects

Within the lifetime of one generation the world has witnessed the decline, or the near extinction of a way of life of nomadic societies. The tribal lore of pastoral societies who roamed across thousands of kilometers with their great herds already belongs to history. In many areas whole communities have been forced to give up a way of life practiced for generations. Adjusting to newer ways of life has not been easy for them. Psychological and emotional scars from the rapidity of change will require more than a generation to heal.

Whereas the great migrations of the colonial era were essentially large-scale exodus from Europe to new colonies being established in conquered territories or to vacant spaces around the world leading to a demographic transition in Europe, no such luxuries are available to migrating populations in the present day. The migrations of the last 50 years or so—mainly in developing countries—have generally taken place for any of the following reasons: drought; labour movements; scarcities—water, fodder, food, jobs etc.; religious persecutions; forced evictions; eco-compulsions; habitat deterioration; war and so on. These migrations can further be grouped under two broad categories: permanent and semi-permanent.

## Demographic Swamping

The reference here is to demographic swamping as a deliberate state policy to effect changes in the population ratio in a given area. It is distinct from the demographic shifts that take place from time to time due to other factors (dealt with elsewhere in the paper). A prime example of demographic swamping in the second half of the twentieth century—i.e., since the setting up of the United Nations Organisation, after the Second World War—is China.

In the case of China, the swamping of local populations in Tibet and Xinjiang by state-sponsored Han settlers are arguably the most glaring examples in recent times of the use of the demographic tool to further state policy or to quell any prospective urge on the part of the indigenous population to demand greater freedom.

An altogether different type of demographic swamping is taking place in other parts of the world. In some countries, especially in Europe, it results from an aging and declining population. Fast growing populations from across the Mediterranean have been long attracted to the magnet of Western Europe's economic prosperity. There is a possibility of 21st century Europe being again engulfed by successive waves from the south, a case of history repeating itself after more than a millennium. Such fears in the minds of several European demographers are hardly imaginary. Demographic swamping of Europe will inevitably result from declining numbers. It is unavoidable. The population of Italy is expected to fall from 127 million to 105 million by 2050. In France the number of migrants needed to sustain the ratio of working age people to retirees would need to be augmented to 20 to 40 times the annual numbers for the last ten years. In post-war 1950s, Germany's fertility rates were among the lowest at 2.2 births per woman. The rate is expected to decline to 1.64 in 2050.

Further to the east, in the case of the European part of Russia, regardless of the new geo-strategic configurations resulting from the end of the Cold War, the underlying fears in the minds of European Russians of being swamped by Asiatic hordes are never far below the surface.*

Similar population shifts have taken place and are still taking place in the United States of America, where due to the economic disparities with Mexico, and further south, the original European descent settlers could be outnumbered in about five or six decades by the Hispanics. The U.S. estimate of 'documented' migrants from 1990-1996 is 1.1 million per year—more than needed to prevent a decline in the population or in the working-age population.

Conditions of demographic swamping obtain as well within the Indian Union. An appraisal of the insurgency in Tripura brings into focus the fact that insurgency was not born out of any ideological conviction, but was more an expression of the tribals' discontent with the changing demographic profile in favour of non-tribals. At the root of the discontent was the alienation of tribal land. The population of Tripura increased more than twenty-fold in the last century.

* See also quotation on p.141.

There is no authentic figure of illegal migrants from Bangladesh. Indrajit Gupta, the Union Home Minister of the time, stated in Parliament on 6 May 1997, that there were ten million illegal migrants in India out of which nearly four million were in Assam.

## Producing Human Surplus for Economic Exploitation

The business community is not the only class that looks at the burgeoning population as a resource base for cheap labour, oblivious of the environmental degradation caused by this increase in the last century. Many among the economically deprived segments are shrewdly creating human surplus in cynical disregard of the need to exercise restraint, in the light of their experience that the state, global donors as well as nongovernmental organisations have joined hands to prevent the children in the slum clusters from perishing, through well-funded programmes.

The lack of firmness on the part of governments in the face of protest demonstrations orchestrated by vested interests, leads to sale of young girls to septuagenarians and even octogenarians and paedophile rings operating globally. Locally, any number of young children get kidnapped and maimed by organised beggar gangs. In some areas girls are routinely sold into prostitution for pecuniary benefits. In the case of India's neighbours where so-called jehadis run religious institutions to mass produce fanatics for their own political ambitions, it is only parents who have large number of children, i.e., those who have created a surplus, part with their fifth, sixth and seventh child to the religious seminaries. There have been very few cases, if any, from the economically depressed classes where parents with two or three children have offered their boys for jehad.

In the face of such exploitation of children—with the tacit consent of parents—the state becomes a partner in crime and inhumanity if it fails to limit proliferation of population for such anti-social ends.

There is another aspect of proliferating hordes that needs to be taken into account. It devalues human dignity. The quality of life required to maintain a modicum of human dignity becomes almost impossible to sustain when numbers begin to surpass the carrying capacity of the land. Since surpluses automatically connote assets larger than required they tend to be traded off as mere numbers like any other commodity. The purely commercial ideation then gives rise to possibilities of cynical military exploitation at the hands of demagogues.

Chairman Mao, was reported to have often mused that China would be able to sustain a full-scale nuclear exchange because even after losing a few hundred million Chinese people there would be sufficient numbers left over. His successors today may be more circumspect, or more fully cognisant of the fragile state of the planet to entertain such notions. Nevertheless, there remain a few military diehards among them, who to this day have gone on record—maybe only sabre-rattling—to the effect that China could afford to lose ten million people in order to secure Taiwan for future generations of the Peoples Republic of China.

In sharp contrast, countries that have stabilised their populations at manageable levels, or face declining numbers, would be loath to remotely consider such sacrifices of even small numbers for purely military ends—other than for meeting direct military threats to their own societies.

## Consequences of Population Displacements in the Colonial Era

Large-scale population displacements took place in the wake of the Industrial Revolution leading to the European expansions of the eighteenth and nineteenth centuries.

Not only did the European population fan out to settle down in thinly populated areas around the world, they were instrumental in eradicating and displacing sizeable numbers of natives from one area to another for economic exploitation of the conquered territories. The moment the colonial masters left these conquered territories after World War II the newly independent states found it difficult to harmonise with the imported populations of the colonial era. Any number of instances can be given. While Fiji and Sri Lanka can be cited as prime examples there are many more in other parts of the world.

The problem extends, in a modified form, to the population displacements carried out in the Central Asian Republics during the Stalin era in the erstwhile Soviet Union. The legacy of those displacements, effected several decades ago, continues to trouble the region after the melting away of the central authority exercised from Moscow. What the outcome of those policies will be in the decades ahead is difficult to predict. What does emerge, however, is that latent tensions can come to the boil to engender cycles of violence when external agencies attempt to stoke the fires.

In southeast Asia, Indonesia provides a classic example (in the colonial mould) of unforeseen results of state-mandated population displacements. There is sufficient empirical evidence from all around the world to show that the transplanted populations have a different approach to the exploitation of land and the natural resources in the new locations. Their attachment, or reverence, for the natural environment around the new settlements is seldom, if ever as deep as that of the original inhabitants. They generally exploit the land with a ruthlessness that ends up by degrading the environment, to the dismay of the locals. This builds up resentments that keep simmering for years till one day there is a settling of scores again when the central authority that orchestrated the displacements loses its grip on the outlying areas. The internecine killings that erupt manifestly have a religious or ethnic bias. But a deeper examination would show that it is the basic violation by the settlers of the land use patterns being followed earlier by the indigenes whom they have displaced which often becomes the root cause for disharmony.

## Ethnic Cleansing as a Weapon of War

Ethnic cleansing has been taking place since time immemorial. In the Middle Ages, and especially following the Industrial Revolution, the great European expansion into other continents of the world was achieved, to quite an extent, through the extermination of local populations. The most notable examples that come to mind are the near-extermination of the indigenous populations in the Americas and Australia. Since the scope of the paper is to discern recent demographic trends in order to study the demographic dynamic evolving in the twenty-first century, there is a need to concentrate more on present day trends.

Ethnic cleansing is now being increasingly resorted to in several parts of the world where totalitarian regimes hold sway and more so where the judiciary has been subordinated to the governing hierarchy. In the continent of Africa, ethnic cleansing is a legacy of the artificially created state boundaries of nation states consolidated during the colonial era. That is not to say that if European dominion over these lands had not taken place the same populations would have lived in harmony. They might well have exterminated each other in the same manner that is being practiced today.

The matter of the greatest concern to the global community, however, is the religion-inspired ethnic cleansing gaining ground in many parts of the world. The horrors of the Nazi era in Germany can be revisited far more efficiently by even small bands of fanatics due to the increasing lethality and area coverage of modern weapons which have proliferated across the globe. Their easy availability and ease of manufacture compounds the problem.

## Demographic Dynamic: India and the Subcontinent

Recently, a well-known global publication[3] came out with a series of first-rate articles by leading experts on "how to save the earth". On every page the stark reality of human depredations leading to ecological decline was clearly brought out. There has been an explosion of such reportage for several decades and yet in countries like India and its subcontinental neighbours the governing hierarchies follow an ostrich-like policy. Their lack of well-managed population policies has seen the numbers multiplying year in and year out.

And what can the government in India say for the future of all the children it happily represented with such fanfare with the advent of Aastha, the billionth baby? Is it prepared for the increasing number of potential mothers with the population of the females in the reproductive ages of 15-49 years expected to go up to 24 percent by the end of the year 2000? It would be worth recalling a piece from a paper published in 1985, a good 15 years before the birth of Aastha:

- "We have perhaps entered the last decade when we still have the semblance of an option for a reasoned approach to the interrelated problem of over-population and environmental conservation. And should we not succeed, there can be no doubt that by the year 1990 any government, irrespective of its hue, will have to legislate draconian measures to ensure even a mean level of subsistence".*

- "The problem looks insurmountable only because we cannot muster our will to overcome it. We are wrong to believe that (all) people want large families. In many cases it is the male child syndrome and in most others the children merely keep coming along. Sex is no joy for most women in the slums. In fact, many of them, weary of the daily grind, and barely recovering from the last pregnancy, dread the inevitable onslaught of the drunken male. In a male dominated society that semi-starved woman, battered both by fortune and her spouse, would welcome a deliverance from constant childbearing. We have failed to reach her".

The extract was specifically recalled to make the point that as early as the 1980s indications were available that although the desire to have large families may not have significantly abated the fact remained that a large number of pregnancies, especially in the slum clusters of metropolitan cities, were *unwanted pregnancies.* At that time the writer had estimated such unwanted pregnancies to be of the order of 30 percent or so. Today, it can be stated with greater certitude that unwanted pregnancies, at any given time, could be as high as 50 percent. With better management of the programme it should be possible to stabilise the population by the year 2020.

This brings one to the second important statement made in the 1985 paper:

"The family planning programme in India at the end of 1984 suffers not so much from a resistance on the part of the populace to adopt a small family norm, but from organisational infirmity".*

* 'The Population Problem in India' talk delivered by Vinod Saighal at the National Defence College, 16 January 1985.

India now has one billion people, 16 percent of the world's population on only 2.4 percent of the globe's land area, according to the Planning Commission's technical group on population projection. "India's current annual increase in population of 15.5 million is large enough to neutralise any efforts to conserve the resource endowment and environment and may soon make it the most populous country of the world, overtaking China by 2045," says the national population policy, (NPP) 2000 report.

**Percentage of infants with low birth-weights**

| **South Asia** | | **South East Asia** | |
|---|---|---|---|
| Bangladesh | 50 | Indonesia | 14 |
| India | 33 | Laos | 18 |
| Nepal | 26 | Malaysia | 10 |
| Pakistan | 25 | Philippines | 15 |
| Sri Lanka | 25 | Thailand | 13 |
| | | Fiji | 18 |
| | | Vietnam | 17 |

Source: Dr S Gopalan, *NFI Bulletin*, July 1998

India's population grew in the 40 years between 1901 and 1941, the last census before Independence, by approximately 134 percent. Leaving out the decade 1941 to 1951, in which year the first post-Independence census took place, in the 40 years from 1951 to 1991, the population grew by over 233 percent. However, India's land area, rivers, mountains, cultivable land have all remained constant because land is not an elastic resource. No doubt, its productivity can be increased by scientific use, but when there is inexorable pressure of human and cattle population, the speed of exploitation exceeds the speed of recuperation and scientific methods prove insufficient. That is precisely what happened in India. The forest cover shrank not because the people were bent upon destroying the forests, but because there were many more people who had become dependent on the same forest area. Naturally-exerted biotic pressures can lead to more intensive use of forests, with a reduced growing cycle and, therefore, an inadequate opportunity for plant life to regenerate itself. With increased cattle population and a vastly increased human population, this cycle has been truncated and so heavily disturbed that the trees never grow beyond scrappy scrub.

Against a sustainable level of 31 million cow units per annum that might graze in forests, the livestock that grazes in the forest is about 100 million cow units. Shrinkage of grazing land and high grazing pressure per unit land have led to scarcity of feed and fodder for the animals. India's land capacity to support grazing is for approximately 50 million heads of livestock, while the population is 450 million.

..."All of (the) world's people must come fully to terms with the fact that a person's biological right to have children must be mediated by his or her social responsibility not to have too many". J.Kenneth Smail [4]

## The Regional Outlook

The last paragraph from the writer's 1985 paper, referred to earlier, is reproduced below:

- "I would like to end this talk on the population problem in India by placing before you the proposition that I have no doubt that with renewed vigour and professional approach India will yet stabilise it population at manageable levels. However, our neighbours, especially Bangladesh and Pakistan may not be able to do so. For instance, in 1973 these two countries had a crude birth rate of nearly 47, i.e. the same that obtained for undivided India at the end of the last century. To put it mildly the governments of these countries do not appear to be unduly alarmed. I foresee a time when the hungry populations of those countries spill over national frontiers under relentless pressure of unchecked growth and faltering economies. The groundwork for strife in the years ahead is being laid now. We must avert disaster while it can still be averted." *

## Future Projections: The Necessity for Global Action

At the start of the new century there is a distinct need to look at the population dynamic globally, in a holistic manner, freed from the infirmities of the north-south, east-west, rich-poor divides that plagued most global protocols of the last century. It calls for the establishment of a global commission set up at the behest of the UN Secretary General, Director General UNESCO, or the Director-General WHO. The major items on the agenda of the global population commission (GPC)** would include: convention on the displacement of populations, updating of the 1950 refugees convention, protocol on global waste management, demographic extinctions and future ecological hazards. The GPC would be required to consider: legislation, regulation, committee action, institutional practice, legal decisions and the like in the form of binding global protocols and model national legislations.

---

* The 'Population Problem in India' talk delivered by Vinod Saighal at the National Defence College, 16 January 1985.

** A Global Commision on International Migration, co-chaired by distinguished public figures from Sweden and South Africa has been recently established. (Speech by Kofi A. Annan to the European Parliament on 29 January 2004)

See also Managing Migration Better' by Kofi A. Annan, *The Hindu*, 29 January 2004.

See also 'The Demographic Dynamic in the 21st Century' by Vinod Saighal, *World Afffairs* vol. no. 4, October-December 2000.

## Global Convention on Displacement of Populations in the 21st Century

To concerned people around the world the realisation had long dawned that either the world of the twenty-first century lives in harmony as a global community or faces the threat of extinction. In the latter case, if not the physical destruction of humankind, but at least a descent into a form of existence that would be minus the ennobling environment that sustained humans up to the present century. Should that be the case there would be an urgent need to not only stabilise the population of the globe at levels as close to the present as possible, but to reverse it in areas where it had crossed the ecologically sustainable thresholds. In the latter category, the stabilisation—and reversal—would prevent the demographic swamping of the pitiably small remaining virgin tracts around the globe as well as neighbouring states, leading to the types of problems discussed earlier in the paper.

There may remain a moral aspect that could militate against a more vigorous policy towards stabilisation and then reversal of the population growth in overburdened landmasses like the Indian subcontinent, Indonesia and several countries in Africa. Such professions of moral outrage—actual or merely professed—need to be weighed against the de-humanisation that results from the mass deprivation obtaining in the poverty-stricken regions of the world where existence becomes less than sub human, where the ambient environment is one of starvation, squalor and lack of privacy.

There is much more that can be written about the abysmal poverty, human degradation and hopelessness that prevails in areas where the so-called dregs of society live out their lives. The vigorous action recommended does not envisage the draconian policies pursued by the Chinese government to achieve population stabilisation. Although, in the case of China as well, the firmness demonstrated towards the people of the earlier generation to ensure stabilisation has to be weighed against the horrific devastation that has been avoided due to the population of China not touching two billion. Additionally, it has to be weighed against the improved quality of life that has resulted for the present generation in China and for the generations to come. The past sacrifice has led to future benefits of an order of magnitude compared to what the condition would have been if the policy had not been vigorously pursued.

In the case of the subcontinent it is hardly a question of coercive action, especially in India. The 'organisational infirmity' talked about earlier not only remains but has been institutionalised to a greater degree in the most populous BIMARU states. Even if half the unwanted pregnancies were to be avoided India's population would fast reach the stabilisation point. But that is not to be. Ill-conceived, maladministered plans seldom benefit the populations who are supposed to benefit from them. They often end up by exacerbating the situation. That is not to belittle, of course, the phenomenal benefits in the fields of childcare and maternal health that have resulted wherever the programmes were ably administered.

Coming to the declining populations in the mainly affluent societies of the world, a thought needs to be given to managing the transition in a more rational manner to prevent the suppression of diversity and ethnicity a hundred years hence as has happened in the case of the Indian state of Tripura and other such areas in the world where small indigenous populations have been demographically swamped from waves of migrants from other areas. In this regard the European Union could adopt a 'fifty-year demographic stabilisation policy' by methods that do not leave legacies of racial conflicts for coming generations. The first method relates to state crêches where infants are adopted from around the world to be brought up in the culture of host nations *ab initio*. After a given age they would be made available for re-adoption to childless couples, or any other suitable variation. Alternatively, or concomitantly, the concerned states, in anticipation of their shortages in the coming years could decide to increase the annual intake from those regions wherefrom the incoming influx represents populations that would be the most likely to harmonise with the existing cultures. This aspect of harmonisation requires to be carefully analysed. There is a beautiful story dating back to the arrival of Parsis in India over twelve centuries ago. One of the groups of the Zoroastrian diaspora from Persia landed on the western coast of India. Their leader met the local king and asked that his small band be allowed to settle down there. The king had a bowl of milk, which was full to the brim brought to him. He handed it to the leader of the group that sought refuge in his kingdom, to indicate that there was virtually no space left for others to settle down. The leader of the Zoroastrians took some sugar from a pouch and carefully stirred the bowl, taking care not to spill even a drop. The sweetened bowl of milk was respectfully handed back to the king. The enterprising band settled down in the new land. They kept their customs. They have added immensely to the richness of India. Even to this day the most respected names in the fields of industry, philanthropy and scientific research are those of the Parsis.

A thought needs to be given to rising sea-levels and the quantum of people likely to be displaced; as also the areas where such displacement would take place. It may not be always feasible, or desirable, for the neighbouring countries to bear the entire burden. In many societies where democracy has not stabilised and especially where local empowerment has not taken place sudden influx of large numbers can lead to large-scale ecological devastation of the remaining virgin tracts. Hence, the need for global action, because the planetary interest of the twenty first century demands that the remaining virgin tracts the world over be looked at as a global heritage which has to be preserved at any cost. Allied to this would be the fact that the global warming that could be taking place was the result of global profligacy for which no individual set of people should be expected to bear the cost on the basis of their geographical location. Therefore, besides setting up a revolving fund towards future costs of population displacements coming in this category the GPC could recommend anticipatory global planning to obviate the global tensions that would surely arise if such planning were not to be undertaken.

Anticipatory global action will go a long way to ameliorate the misery that could afflict humankind and most species of the animal kingdom on a scale not yet experienced in the twentieth century. In the absence of such action displaced populations of tomorrow might be made second class citizens, almost slaves, on account of the inability of many nations to support larger human populations. It would leave the host nations no choice but to locate the rush of immigrants in World War II type of internment camps to be exploited as cheap labour and fed, sheltered and clothed at minimal subsistence levels—as is already happening in some areas of the world. This would be made easier with modern technology with the issuance of identity cards.

India becomes an interesting case study for the increased population influx from the north, south, east and west in the coming years. Either it regards the anticipated increase as human waste and treats the new arrivals accordingly or plans to take on the anticipated burden in a humane manner. Had India not been partitioned when the British left, the problem would still have had to be addressed by India as the sole subcontinental entity. However, until the time that the nations of the subcontinent continue to act irresponsibly by planning to swamp India with their unwanted human surplus—so much for humanity—India would be fully justified in taking certain measures that do not push the country itself to the brink of disaster.

Such measures could include temporary relocation in designated camps and obliging the refugees to conform to the overall population stabilisation goals of the host country, i.e. to forego the luxury of more than one or two children. Failing which, they would continue to be quarantined, not given employment and deported at the first available opportunity. Not only in the case of inter-country demographic swamping, steps of this type may have to be taken by city councils of urban conglomerates already bursting at the seams and yet facing continuous onslaught of new arrivals by the tens of thousands. (For example, in spite of having reached a population of 14 million, Delhi is still being swamped with an annual influx of half a million). Universal guidelines of this nature, for regions of the world where stabilising the population were to become an acknowledged priority, may have to be agreed to, in principle, at global conventions. While the principle of human rights as the overarching principle for the regulation of global societies would retain its primacy, local modifications necessitated by the inability of host societies to physically accommodate the influx has to be appreciated. The broad agreements could bring in an element of reasonableness into these discussions between societies that have to actually bear the brunt and people who merely remain professional campaigners, at one remove. The guidelines would be applicable for 50 years or till a modicum of population stabilisation were to be achieved.

## Demographic Extinction

Along with the need to attempt a balance between the carrying capacity of the planet is the need to retain the diversity and ethnicity of populations threatened with extinction, mainly due to the destruction of habitats or due to ethnic cleansing or demographic swamping. For example, the Chinese government should voluntarily agree to a moratorium on further Han-isation of the Tibetan Plateau. The Chinese recourse to the measures taken would be tantamount to India attempting to solve the Sri Lankan problem, once and for all, by allowing a few million Tamils to be pushed across the Palk Straits to demographically swamp the Sinhala population, over a period of time.

Another type of danger of extinction stems from the chemical pollution of the planet and from unregulated, little understood long-term effects of genetic modification of species. Hormone disrupting chemicals are reported to be reducing the sperm count of Japanese males. Over a period of time it could have serious effects on the future of Japanese society. There would likely be other such effects taking place in areas where research facilities do not exist or exist in an elementary form or do not constitute a priority in the face of more pressing problems of day to day survival. Future demographic hazards arising from testing of more lethal weapons by the militaries of the world—depleted uranium weapons being an example—need to be brought into the purview of global protocols to control, limit or ban such research. Rising toxicity levels will lead to malformation in children and so many other species. Sadly, the other species are hardly ever given a thought to.

## Waste Management

Many countries are increasingly discovering that their rivers have become polluted, in some cases almost beyond redemption. Again taking the case of India, there was an almost 840 percent increase in urban population between 1901 and 1991. Cities are now eight-and-a-half times more crowded than they were in 1901. With such unplanned, unmanageable, constantly increasing concentrations of populations, services in the matter of water supply and sewerage and both off-take of water and discharge of effluents and garbage reach such proportions that the waterways run empty, and sewage and garbage pollute both the land and water. One of the more poignant cases relates to the Sabarmati Ashram of Mahatma Gandhi. What a contrast between the description of the Mahatma's abode redolent with fragrant breezes wafting from the river's bank when he dwelt there and the stench emanating from the sewer that now trickles past the Ashram walls. The increasing demand for land for various urban activities results in greenfield areas being brought under construction, thus permanently devastating land, which in the past was under cyclical use as per the dictates of nature. Every third river system or stream is now turning into a sewer, permanently destroying the ecology of the land. Worse is the case of the beautiful hill stations of yore, now wilting under unsupportable population pressures.

Waste management problems are afflicting societies both rich and poor across the world, each municipality, megapolis and region managing as best as they can without a care for the effects of such wastefully destructive profusion on the global landscape. Here too there is a need for a global convention on waste management. One of the best remedies still available being the reduction of human population pressures.

## Concluding Remarks

The population explosion is now adding nearly the equivalent of China's population every ten years or so to the planet, changing the very nature of planetary land use to the detriment of almost every beautiful thing worth preserving on the planet. The subcontinent remains one of the biggest offenders in this regard. The people of this wasting landmass should realise that not even a major nuclear exchange between the two subcontinental adversaries will reverse the relentless growth of the human mass. A few tens of millions perishing no longer represent a significant percentage at this belated stage. Actually that many people will not die. Instead there would be a few hundred million sub-human, genetically deformed, malnourished people hobbling around on the landscape between Kabul, Karachi and Calcutta. People make decisions about family size based on present needs and do not realise that growth rate of 3 percent per year, if continued for a century, would lead to a nineteen-fold multiplication of the population. The leaders of the subcontinent must pose themselves the question:

"Are they (by their inaction) well on the way to spawning a race of mentally retarded and under-developed people in this ancient land which once boasted of exceptional mental faculties; faculties that provided mankind with the most illuminating insights on the very nature of existence"?

The destruction of planetary diversity in the twentieth century has taken on an added frenzy in the twenty-first. The future of the coming generations of humans and animal kind—whichever species that might still be around—is being destroyed by the cancerous growth of the prolific procreators, the beastly humans. Unwilling, for even a brief span of time, to consider putting a slight curb on their exponentially multiplying (selfish) needs. They have ceased caring that pesticides applied to agricultural fields may show up in ground water 10 years later and cause cancer 30 years later—the profits being 'here and now'. The more the overproduction of children the more intensive the use of fertilizers and pesticides in the developing world.

The world must look dispassionately at the global dimension of the problem, which, if it remains unchecked for just a few more decades, will herald an end to most of the natural beauty of the planet that can still be perceived in parts by the present generation of humans. A debate has been raging in many parts of the world on human needs versus animal needs. The human species is proliferating exponentially. A few more or less of this particular species will not impoverish the planet. The disappearance of a unique habitat or an endangered species will.

## End Notes

1. *The Statesman,* 5 May 2000.
2. TIME, 29 May 2000.
3. TIME, April-May 2000.
4. *Political and the Life Sciences,* September 1977.

# Index